To:

From:

Life will give you what you ask for so...

Nine steps for making your Life
extraordinary!

If reality can destroy dreams,
then dreams can destroy reality.
Conway Stone

Dream High!
Nine steps for making your life extraordinary.

Copyright © 1999 by Conway Stone
Add this to what you know and give give give.

Published by Dream Enterprises Publications
Conway Stone
500 Briar Hill Road
Louisville, Kentucky 40206-3010
1-888-899-5353
www.dreamhigh.com

Book Cover &Cartoons
Created by Dean Nicklas

ISBN 0-9673165-0-2

Printed in the United States of America

Dedication

This book is dedicated to the one who
has helped me more than any other, the
one who trusts me, who believes in me and
who has allowed me to dream high. I owe
it all to my wife, Polly.

TABLE OF CONTENTS

"The dull boring defeated life, takes the same time and energy as the exciting, life-giving, extraordinary life. Choose always the latter."

From the ancient text

Introduction

It has been 4 years since publishing my first book, "Follow Your Dreams." I have relished and been grateful to God for the success. The book has received the endorsements of two of my heroes, Dr. Denis Waitley and Dr. Robert Schuller. Where the average business book sells 5,000 copies, "Follow Your Dreams" has sold 40,000 copies. Currently it is scheduled to be published in Poland, India and the Czech Republic.

As nice as these accolades are, they are not my best accomplishment. I am most proud of the letters I have received from people who have changed their lives by following their dreams. A young man wrote me from a prison in Missouri asking for a copy of my book because he wanted to use the ideas of my book when he got out of prison. A young lady with multiple sclerosis sat down with her husband and read my book night after night and dreamed of opening an art studio. Today, the LionHeart Art Studio is open and successful in Louisville Kentucky. I received a letter from another young lady who heard me speak about a difficult time in my life I call the flood. She wrote to say she had been in her own flood for several years and needed to hear about how to change her thinking and get beyond the high water.

These are the trophies I cherish and the reason I continue to speak and write. It is for these people and for you that I write "Dream High!"

Conway

Section I

Dream High!!!

"Immigrants are 4 times more likely to become millionaires than people born in this country."

Zig Ziglar

The difference is...**The Dream!**

"Within two years, they pay cash for a 3 bedroom home!" Edgardo said.

"You must be joking," I retorted trying to pick my chin up off the floor.

"No. It's true. When an immigrant from Bosnia, Cuba or Albania comes to live in these apartments, they begin working immediately and within 2 or 3 years they move out of these apartments and pay cash for a 3 bedroom brick home." Edgardo Mansilla is a social worker at the Americana Apartment Complex[1] in Louisville Kentucky. He was explaining all of this to me as if it were an ordinary occurrence, like it was no big deal.

"Well, that's amazing!" I exclaimed. **"Only in America."**

"Yea, but it's not the whole story," Edgardo challenged.

"Oh really! Well, tell me the rest," I said with a smile on my face expecting to hear some more exciting news.

"Well, we have a number of American families move in here. People born in this country with education and good backgrounds. When these American families move into these apartments they stay 2 or 3 years also, but when they move out, they move to another apartment complex. They don't move up, they just move on." I could see the sadness in Edgardo's eye as he slowly shook his head.

---

[1]The Americana Apartment complex is a 2,000 person apartment complex housing a mix of ethnic groups, immigrants and refugees. 17 languages are spoken there.

What is the difference?

What's the difference between the immigrant paying cash for a 3 bedroom brick home and the American moving to another apartment?

The difference is not time. Both the American and the immigrant have 24 hours a day. The difference is not talent. Both the American and the immigrant have talent and in fact the American has more tangible talent in this case because they know the English language and the American economic system.

The difference is not desire. If you ask most people they desire similar things: nice job, house and car and a great future for their kids. The difference is not opportunity: both people live in America. The same opportunities at McDonalds, dry cleaners and restaurants are available both for the immigrant and the American.

The difference is the dream! The immigrant has his or her eyes set on a very high dream. They believe their dream can come true and develop clear plans to work toward their dream.

The Americans on the other hand have their eyes focused on the circumstances of their lives. And they allow the realities of their circumstances to destroy their dreams.

The question comes, "Which one of these people do you want to be?" Do you want to be like the immigrant setting and **accomplishing** very high almost impossible dreams or do you want to be like the others in this story who have let people, life and circumstances kill their dreams and keep on trudging on in their same old ruts?

The biggest difference between the two is where do you have your eyes set? Are your eyes, heart, soul and energy focused on your dreams or are they focused on the mundane circumstances of your day to day existence?

I stood there dumbfounded, in shock really, with my eyes bugged out and my mouth gaping open as Edgardo spoke. The thought kept running through my mind... "If an immigrant who cannot speak English can come to this country with nothing but the clothes on his/her back, face all of the difficulties of language, prejudice, harsh economic forces and win, what the heck is stopping me?!! Why isn't my house paid off? Why am I not earning $250,000 a year? Why am I not traveling to Europe twice a year? The answer is simple. I'm not dreaming high enough!

This is going to change in my life. The immigrant has taught me that Life will give you what you ask for; so it's time for me to ask more of Life. It's time for me to dream higher! What about you?

You are a Dreamer!!

There was a blockbuster movie out several years ago entitled 'Natural Born Killers.' It portrayed a couple crazy enough to kill and destroy everything they touched. There are people who believe all of us are born killers by nature. I have but one thing to say about this "bunk."

We are not natural born killers. **We are natural born dreamers**. By nature we have the ability to envision a new reality and make that vision (or dream) come true. Let me give you a simple example.

Do you remember when you were in the second grade and you dreamed of a new bicycle? You remember the color and style and how much it cost? Mine was silver with a banana seat and high backrest and those long strings flowing from the handle bars. Yours might have been red or blue with a bell or a basket attached. We are natural born dreamers from way back then.

The dreaming did not stop there. You had other childhood dreams. Perhaps you had dreams of owning a football all your own or dreamed of owning a favorite Barbie doll. You dreamed of going to camp or making the basketball team. Much of our play as children is dreaming. I dreamed a great deal of being a wide receiver with the Minnesota Vikings of the National Football League. Some ladies may have dreams of being Mary Lou Retton or a high school cheerleader. When we get into high school, often we dream of graduation, going to college, getting a car, getting a job, etc.

This seeing a vision of our future and working to make it come true is the dreaming process and it is the natural state of people.

My Story

Like you I was born a natural dreamer. I remember my 5th birthday when I was asked to make a wish and blow out the candles. I silently wished a brand new drum set would magically appear in my room. So I blew out the candles and before the cake was even cut, I ran up to my room to see if the drum set was there. The set was not there of course, but this did not stop this young dreamer.

As I grew older I remember the dreams of being a good fisherman, a good hunter, of owning a motorcycle and even of being a wide receiver for the Minnesota Vikings. And one by one these dreams came true. I did become a good hunter and fisherman. I did learn to play the drums and played in high school and college. I even bought a motorcycle when I was 16 and still enjoy riding to this day. I will admit I never did play organized football something I still regret, but I still have a passion for Vikings football and I have relished their advancements in recent years.

Over the years I have wondered where this passion for dreaming has come from. My family background may be very similar to yours. See if you notice any similarities.

I was born in the small town of Paragould nestled in the delta flat land of Northeast Arkansas. Paragould at that time had a population of 9,500 people and was a cotton mill town, trading post and railroad stop for Greene county Arkansas. My father became a minister when I was 5 years of age and we lived in even smaller towns as he began his career. We moved to the birthplace of Johnny Cash, Kingsland Arkansas with a population at that time of 216 people. Then we moved to a rural part of Kentucky to a town with a population of 45 people.

To this day my grandparents and mother live just outside Marmaduke Arkansas which is just south of Piggot Arkansas. Yes, like many people in this nation I came from very humble beginnings.

At the same time the culture in which I was born was very rich. My family was very dedicated to God, family and telling the truth. We had a rich tradition of singing, joke telling and most of all story telling. But my family was very rich in another way. I came from a long line of forward thinking Americans who believe that life and people could get better.

My father always tells the story of him and my grandfather visiting a group of old men sitting around the courthouse steps and the conversation turned to the old southern tradition of saying how bad things are today and how good the old days were. "If we could just go back to the good old days, then we would be better off." On the way home my grandfather said to my father, "Son, what are those guys talking about? Back in the so-called 'good old days,' people died of whooping cough, pneumonia, and polio. We didn't have electricity and hardly any money to speak of and most of us had to walk to work if we had any work at all. How do they get by with saying that things were better? Today most everything is better, from the flow of money, to the houses we live in, to screens on the front door. I can assure you the '67 Chevrolet is far better than the '37 Packard." Grandpa believed life was getting better and each of us could improve.

Grandpa not only talked about this belief he also lived it in his own life. Having been born on a farm and grown up with very little formal education, Grandpa was struck with undulate fever that left him bedridden much of his life. Nevertheless Grandpa moved his family to the small town and began studying carpentry and electrician skills through mail order books at night. It took a while, but eventually he became a licensed carpenter and a licensed electrician and he remodeled houses for a living. One by one he bought and rented houses and eventually owned an entire city block. At his retirement he owned and rented 7 houses and had a very comfortable retirement at a time when many people his age barely scraped by on social security.

I was fortunate enough to inherit a couple of his original mail order study books. I have them prominently displayed in my office to remind me of where I came from and that life can get better.

My grandpa Buchanan on my mother's side also helped me with this spirit of improving. One hot day in June he and I were working on my car. Standing there on the gravel outside his home,

I was really battling whether I should stay near my family in rural Arkansas or move hundreds of miles away to Louisville Kentucky where I had made some friends and knew I could improve my education. Grandpa asked me what I was planning to do with my life and I told him I was thinking about moving to Louisville, but was really torn about what to do. Grandpa turned to me and said, "Conway, I believe a man should go anywhere he can better himself." It's funny how clear the truth can be sometimes. In one sentence, my Grandfather gave me permission to follow my dreams and he passed on this spirit that life can get better.

This was the culture I was fortunate enough to grow up in and I could tell you many other stories of people seeking to improve their lives. I could tell of my father leaving his life as a salesman to be the first in his family to get a college education. I could tell you of my father-in-law who at age 14 urged his father to buy a better grade of cattle which in turn improved the herd and the family business. I could tell you of dairy farmers I worked for who improved their barns so they could do their business more efficiently. This idea of envisioning a better future and working to make that dream a reality is the story of my people and indeed the story of all America. These men and women taught me to be a dreamer.

Dreamers lose their way.

As I travel and speak around the nation I am astonished at the number of sharp intelligent professionals who come up to me and say, "I have no dreams." This has really bothered me to see such talent going to waste. So I began to study and research the problem and here's what I found. The problem is not that we're not dreamers, the problem is we have accomplished our dreams.

Think about this - when you graduated from high school, what were your dreams? You dreamed of going to college, getting married, getting a good job, living in a decent house and driving a decent car. Haven't you already accomplished those dreams? Most of us in middle class America either did or did not attend college moving us past this dream, we settled the issue of marriage and most of us live in decent houses, have decent jobs and drive decent cars. We may not have them paid for yet, but we are living our dreams!

The person who has accomplished their dreams and the person with no dreams have the same problem. They are often stuck, bored and stagnated. Is it any wonder so many people in our society run to the latest fad, whether it is the latest blockbuster movie, a new trend in clothes, a new brand of car or soft drink or even the Internet? Some people turn to drugs, sex or alcohol just to get some feeling or excitement into their lives, because there is no dream, no drive, no passion to follow. Although we may love our spouses, our kids and our job, often we repeat the line from the old song, "Is that all there is?"

The answer to this boredom or stagnation is not escapism or following the crowd. The answer is to tap into the genius we have inside, to recapture our natural state as dreamers, to dream high and to turn those dreams into reality. This *you* can do if you will dare to dream high!

This dreamer has also lost his dream occasionally. When it came time to attend college, I had three dreams I wanted to accomplish. First I wanted to get a degree in psychology so I could become a Christian psychologist, second I wanted to live overseas so I could learn about the world and people from another culture, and third I wanted to find the young lady I would marry. These very clear concrete dreams did their job. They gave me a picture to move toward, they gave me something very concrete to do and when I got bored or lost, just remembering these dreams got me back on track.

And like most dreams we set, 5 years later I had far exceeded my expectations. During what would have been my senior year I was invited to travel to Nigeria Africa as an exchange student and lived there for one school year. Doing this allowed me to turn my double major into two college degrees - one in Religion and one in Psychology. The third dream did not come true as I had envisioned. I did not find the young lady I would marry in college, but a few years later I met a beautiful redhead by the name of Polly and this past May we celebrated our eighth wedding anniversary.

However, when I got out of college I had a serious problem. I had accomplished my dreams and like many people, I had a real problem coming up with new clear dreams that excited me about my future. Consequently, I spent years wandering around trying to find my way. I spent a year in Texas trying to go to graduate school. When that didn't work, I moved to Louisville Kentucky to attend a different graduate school. I tried working with my father in the real estate business. I even spent another year overseas in Tokyo Japan.

It was during this year in Japan that I found my way. I began working with a psychologist who turned me on to some tapes by Dr. Robert Schuller and Dr. Denis Waitley. These men instructed me to write down in clear detail every dream I would like to accomplish. The question Dr. Schuller asked was, "If the world were perfect, if you had all the time in the world and all the money in the world, what would you do? What would you do if you knew you could not fail?"

This ignited my imagination! I dreamed of owning 100 acres of land. I dreamed of starting my own business and I dreamed of starting a non-profit organization. I dreamed of being a millionaire. I dreamed of becoming a philanthropist and giving money away every year. I wrote every detail of these dreams down in a notebook complete with pictures and a plan of action. And I was laughing the entire time, because it was a big joke. I had just been through a bankruptcy with some business dealings. I had been forced to live on borrowed money and when my contract in Japan ended, I would be unemployed. Many people face difficult times in their lives being broke, unemployed and living on borrowed money and this was one of those times for me.

But once again the dreams worked! When I returned to the U.S., I had a sense of purpose. I first went to work as a stockbroker earning money to accomplish my dreams, but while there, the stocks I found most exciting to sell were the upstart companies. Instead of selling the old stodgy stocks that everyone else was selling, I sold the dreams of young companies. Later while working in the financial planning field, I found myself helping people dream of and plan for sending their kids to college and their retirement. Within 6 years of starting with nothing, I had paid off my debts, started my own speaking business, founded a non-profit organization and even jumped off the side of a mountain in a hang-glider.

Today I am still dreaming. With the completion of this my second book, I already have 2 more books I plan to write. I have dreams of directly helping 50,000 people a year follow their dreams. And I have dreams of traveling and speaking in Poland, the Czech Republic and India.

Where are You...

The more important question is where are you? I believe you were born to dream. From the dream of your first bicycle to the dream of going to summer camp, to the dream of the person you would marry, **you are a dreamer!**

Yet many of us forget we are dreamers. This book was written to help you recapture the dreamer inside you. You may be a young person wondering what your future will be. You may be a young couple just starting out in marriage. You may be someone who has just started a new business. You may have lost your dreams in the busyness and drudgery of everyday life. You may have had your dreams stolen by so many well-intentioned people. You may be a little older facing children leaving the house or a career change or even looking toward retirement. You may be on the verge of retirement wondering what you will do with the second half of your life. (Yes, I said second half. That was not a misprint.) Please understand no matter where you are, you are more than you think you are, you can achieve far more than you realize and you can dream higher than you ever thought possible!

"*What lies behind you and what lies ahead of you pales in comparison to what lies within you.*"
Unknown

Step 1
Know Your Genius!

Did you see the movie "Little Man Tate" by Jodie Foster? Jodie played a young waitress who dances at a local bar, smokes two packs of cigarettes a day, drives a worn out Ford and hangs around with a rough rough crowd. This young lady has born to her a child with an IQ of 165.

Can you get the picture? This young genius is born into a very crass mundane world of cigarettes, booze, worries about rent, school bullies and will anyone come to my birthday party?

I truly believe this is a picture of you and me. We are geniuses born into crass mundane worlds. The power of the human brain and spirit is far above any machine currently produced and far above any philosophy we currently know. Yet too many of us walk around using our greatness to mow lawns, wash dishes, and pay rent.

It's the human spirit that gave us the computer, penicillin, sky-scrapers and the cars we drive. A mind very similar to yours gave us the international banking system, the interstate highway system and the Internet.

You see most people born in this world are born with IQ's of somewhere between 110 and 113. I know there are exceptions - people born with lower IQ's and the Mensa society members who claim an average IQ of 148. But for the most part, the average person walking around is born with an IQ between 108 and 115 with most of us in the 110 to 113 area.

And if the truth be told many of the great companies, systems and value created in this world are created by ordinary people like you and me who have found a way to tap greatness within themselves.

Alexander Hamilton, who created the Federal Reserve System that has allowed our currency to be stable and healthy for 215 years, was a person very much like you and me. His IQ was within the same range as ours, yet he created a brilliant system that has made a true difference in our world.

Henry Ford was by his own admission an average person. He used to brag that he was the least educated person on his board. Yet he took the automation process invented by someone else and applied it to an invention called the car that was also invented by someone else and created the Ford Motor company. Some historians credit him with inventing the middle class, because he dared to pay his workers enough money so they could afford to buy his cars. The same can be said about Jack Welch, chairman of GE, or the founder of Prudential or the founder of Coca-Cola. Ordinary people founded McDonalds, Papa Johns Pizza and General Motors.

I know that the person sitting in your chair, holding this book and reading these words has this same type of genius inside. Maybe you have recognized it in gifted people such as artists or musicians or sports figures. Yet many of us are geniuses when it comes to computers, working with children, getting projects completed, being good parents or coaching young people. Yes, greatness can be found in each of us no matter how ordinary our abilities seem. We need to find ways to move beyond our mundane crass worlds and tap the power and greatness within us. One way to let this greatness soar is to tap into the power of dreaming and let our dreams take our spirits higher.

Profiles of Three Dreamers

1. Ann was born and raised in Cleveland Ohio. Her father was a steel worker and her mother a housewife. At 27, Ann found herself working as an assistant manager at a Friendlies Ice Cream Shop. She had been working for Friendlies for 10 years when one day she had a revelation. "Is this what I'm going to do? Flip burgers all my life? I don't want to go this way and I changed." It was at that moment Ann decided to pursue her dream of becoming a nurse."I like working with people and when someone is sick, you go in and do anything f or them and they really appreciate it. That makes you feel good. I mean they can't pay you enough to have that feeling." After two years of school, Ann is just one year away from becoming a registered nurse. She hopes to specialize in obstetric care after a couple years of work.

2. Karen Smiley, a farmer in Maine, could not fine comfortable gloves that fit her hands and lasted through the tough work she faced on the farm. She concluded that all the glove manufacturers were making gloves for men. So, in thinking about her own needs, she began a company called Womanswork that manufactures gloves especially for women. Not the flowered gloves sold in checkout lines, but gloves that farmers, construction women and others can use. Today her company produces gloves for the U.S. Park Service and construction companies all over the world.

3. Mohamed Diop, 53, was born in Senegal. He worked for Citicorp in West Africa for 13 years and decided to come to America to start his own business. Homeland Fashions imports Afrocentric items especially for African Americans and African immigrants. Homeland Fashions' items include $200 suits and $8 ball caps. His sales are expected to reach **$6,000,000 this year.**

"*Be careful what you set your heart on,*
for it will surely be yours."
Ralph Waldo Emerson

Step 2
Find Your Dreams!

I have two nieces who have just entered their teenage years 13&17. I love to ask them the following two questions: "What are you doing?" and "Where are you going?" Can you guess the answers I get from these teenagers?

"What are you doing?" The answer, **"Nothing."**

"Where are you going?" You guessed it, **"Nowhere."**

If you ask most Americans these days the same questions you will get the same answers. Where are you going? Nowhere. What are you doing? Nothing. We are doing a lot of things with family and business. But, few of us have a clue about the big picture of where we are going and why. How did we get in this shape? Well, I believe there are 3 reasons.

1. Many of us have bought the dreams of our family or culture. We have followed the dreams everyone else dreams without taking a serious look at what *we* want to do. The dreams of marriage, college, job and cars are fine, if they are what we want, but if they are simply the dreams others envisioned for us, then our life becomes especially difficult. I see so many people who are simply lost because they are saddled with low-paying dull-but-steady jobs, mortgages, credit card debt beyond their control and kids they love, but the kids have trapped them into years of obligations they did not foresee. There is nothing wrong with these dreams if they are what you choose. There is a serious problem if we simply fall into the path everyone else has followed.

2. As we discussed earlier, we have accomplished the dreams we set out for ourselves. We have the car, the house, the good job and we keep asking the question "now what?" If you find yourself stagnated, bored and unmotivated, ask yourself very seriously if you have accomplished your dreams. Do you have a clear, practical dream you know you can achieve that will propel you into the future? If you don't, start small. Find a small dumb dream you want to accomplish in the next hour even if it is nothing more than a 6-

minute walk or finishing a letter. Success breeds success. Now write down a dream you want to accomplish before the day ends. If you can't think of anything, how about doing 3 push-ups? Yes, they are small dreams, but they will get you moving in the right direction.

3. We seek easy tangible dreams. Many people I know seek dreams of cars or vacation trips to Hawaii. There is nothing wrong with this - it is good and healthy. But once we buy the car or take the trip to Hawaii, the question still comes "is that all there is?" The answer here is to follow dreams that will bring more meaning to life.

4. Many of our dreams have been beaten to death by the people around us and by the systems we live in. Society needs a lot of middle class people and often the systems in our society will dull our dreams to the point of keeping us in our place. We are motivated to keep working, but we are not encouraged to move beyond our current place in society. Friends often do this also. If you have a great idea or dream, they will scoff and tear it down, just to keep you at the same level as them.

Now is the time to get past these difficulties. Now is the time to claim the dreams we want for ourselves. Although you may have asked this question a thousand times, look at it again. Take a look at the dreams you would like to accomplish with the time God has given you here on earth. Write down three answers to that question...

If the world were perfect, if you had all the time in the world, if you had all the money in the world and you knew you could not fail, what would you do?

1. _____

_____

2. _____

_____

3. _____

_____

Congratulations! You have just taken a step that 90% of the people of this world never get around to. Many people claim to have dreams in their minds, but few take the time to write them down. (If the lines above this paragraph are blank...STOP NOW! Write down 3 dreams.)

Profiles of Three Dreamers

1. David Marcheschi as a college student had trouble staying awake to study. He hated the taste of coffee and soda so he looked for a drink with caffeine but no offensive taste. He could not find one. So, he invented Water Joe, a bottled water loaded with caffeine. In 1996, Water Joe was shipping 400,000 bottles a week and earning $12,000,000 in sales. Look to your own needs. This is a great way to find entrepreneurial ideas.

2. Don Douglass of Alamo Group, Inc. is the dominant player in the business of making grass grow along highways. This niche business grossed $190,000,000 this year. His advice to young entrepreneurs, "You don't have to discover the next Netscape. Just find a corner of a market and dominate it."

3. Julia Wales is a member of the Immaculate Heart of Mary Catholic Church. She won a contract from HUD to build 24 apartments and operate them for low income people. HUD chipped in $1.8 million and the houses made a tremendous difference in her community.

"We all have two choices. We can make a living
or we can design a life."
Jim Rohn

Step 3
Design the perfect life!

A minister I know recently bought a new car. Like most Americans he looked at Chevrolets, Fords, Hondas and Toyotas. He eventually paid $18,500 for a very fine maroon 4-door Toyota Corolla.

A couple of months later I got to looking around and realized each of my cars had over 150,000 miles on them. So I set out on the idea of buying another car, and like my pastor friend and most Americans I looked at Chevrolets, Fords, Hondas and Toyotas. Then I got to thinking ... "This is boring. This is what everyone else does. Maybe I should take my own advice and ask the question, "What would I do if I knew I could not fail?"

Well, if you want to know the truth, if money were no object, if I knew I could not fail, I would own a top-of-the-line Mitsubishi 3000GT with a twin turbo engine, leather seats and power everything. Wow! What a dreamer!

There is only one problem with this dream. A 1998 top-of-the-line 3000GT costs $46,700. If I had 46,000 dollars, I don't think I would put it on 4 wheels and drive it down the interstate. But that is my dream. If I knew I could not fail, that is the car I would drive.

So I took the dream seriously and held off buying a car. I took a trip to the only Mitsubishi dealership in Louisville and test drove a new 3000GT. Then I started researching the papers and trade journals. I talked to my knowledgeable friends and my insurance company. I found a full color advertisement and put it over the desk in my office. But because of the expense, I never really believed I would be able to buy one of these cars.

Then one day, while looking through the paper, I saw it - a 1992 Mitsubishi 3000GT. I called and found a young architect needed to buy a house and could not afford to own this car and buy a house at the same time. From the moment I saw this forest green beauty come out of the garage, I knew it belonged to me.

I bought a top-of-the-line forest green Mitsubishi 3000GT with leather seats, a twin turbo engine, power everything and virtually a brand new car with 27,000 original miles for $14,900!!

And the question comes, "What is the difference between me buying my dream car and my pastor friend buying a Toyota?" The difference is not education, we both have advanced degrees. The difference is not will or desire, we both needed and got a car. The difference is not belief, neither of us believed we could afford a 3000GT. The difference is not even money! I paid less for my 3000GT than he paid for his Toyota! The difference, the only difference, is the dream! The only difference is where you have your eyes set!

So one of my friends saw me getting out of this car and asked me if I was going through a mid-life crisis. (The scoffers always abound.) I simply told him the story of my dream and it coming true. Someone standing next to us said, "He lives a charmed life." To which I retorted, **"NO! I live a designed life."**

And another question comes, "If you are going to dream a life, why not dream the best life possible?" Why not design and live an extraordinary life? It takes the same time and energy to live an exciting, creative, abundant and meaningful life as it does to live an average life. The factory line worker, the housewife and the executive all work 8 or 10 hours a day and fight the same battles of family, cars and health. The only difference is the design of their lives.

Your life can be designed anyway you wish it to be, so, start today designing the extraordinary life. Instead of dreaming of a regular car or an ordinary house, why not set your sights on your dream car and your dream house? Instead of having an ordinary marriage, why not dream and design the best marriage? Can you add more meaning and depth to your life with your family, hobbies, ideas and volunteer work? It may take a few years to achieve these dreams but dreams do come true and the reward is well worth it! Set your eyes on the higher dreams and work toward them.

The Dreams of your life.

Let's take a look at some dreams that will help you design an extraordinary life.

1. Career. You will spend close to 1/3 of your life working and it is important that your work be enjoyable. What would be your perfect job? I have been collecting some dream jobs that prove to me you can design any life and job you wish. Maybe these would inspire your thinking about careers ....

1. David Ingram is a personal shopper for the rich & famous. He spends millions of dollars a year buying gifts for celebrities like Elizabeth Taylor, Michael Jackson and Dolly Parton. Many stores wine and dine him just like they would a celebrity and he earns around $150,000 a year doing what he loves. Could you live this type of lifestyle?

2. Elaine Farley earns $100,000 a year as the editor of the Sports Illustrated swimsuit edition. 30 weeks a year, she travels to beautiful beaches all over the world supervising the photography of beautiful women in thin bikinis with ocean water splashing over them. Since I am married and my mother will read this book, let me say emphatically, **I have no idea who would want such a job,** but perhaps this job will illustrate that anything is possible and will inspire you to seek the career of your choice.

3. Michael Ferraro has the unbelievable job of taste tester for Godiva Chocolatier. Can you believe this? He is paid thousands of dollars a year to eat 1/2 pound of chocolate a day. This is my dream job!

4. Comic book artist Todd McFarlane earns $5,000,000 a year writing comic books! Yes, you could do this.

5. Mark Rolfing teaches beginning golf in Honolulu Hawaii. He gives lessons about 6 hours a day and spends the rest of his time pursuing his own golf game.

6. Mrs. Olea runs the "By Faith Guest House" in Bermuda. She enjoys the world's most perfect weather and meets people from all over the world. Not a bad life. I met Mrs. Olea on a recent trip to Bermuda. She does live in a beautiful part of the world.

If you could design the perfect life what would be your dream career? What would you do if you knew you could not fail?

_____

_____

_____

_____

_____

2. Debt Free. Would not an extraordinary life include living debt free? How much would you have to pay off to be totally debt free? Including all mortgages. Dave Ramsey, author of the book "Financial Peace," is fond of saying, "the new status symbol is not the BMW but a paid-off mortgage."

_____

_____

_____

Now set as a goal to eliminate all debt. Take your list and put all extra money to paying off the smallest debt first. Then pay off the second smallest and then the third smallest. You can take on an extra job to make extra payments and use all freed up money to pay against the next debt.

3. Income. If you could name the total income you would like your family to bring home what would that income be?

Remember income would include your salary, your spouse's salary, investment income, rental income, hobby income, income from a second job, etc.

4. Net Worth. What net worth would you like to obtain over the next 3 years?

_____

_____

5. Place to Live. If you could live in any part of the country, would you move from where you are living now?   In what country, city or area would you live?

_____

_____

_____

An Extraordinary Life would entail some fun stuff, wouldn't it?

6. Name 6 of the greatest places in the world you would like to travel to.
　　1.
　　2.
　　3.
　　4.
　　5.
　　6.

7. Name 6 of the craziest places you'd like to visit.
　　1. Timbuktu
　　2. SEE Rock City
　　3.
　　4.
　　5.
　　6.

8. Name 6 crazy things you'd like to do.

1. Sky dive
2. Hang glide
3.
4.
5.
6

9. What would be the coolest thing you could ever do? Play sax in a band? Act in a play or a movie? Drive cross country? Run for public office?

_____

_____

_____

10. Have you ever had an invention idea you thought would be perfect for the world? What is it? Write it in as much detail as you can.

_____

_____

_____

11. Have you ever had a book idea or a title for a book you thought would help a lot of people or make you a lot of money? Describe it...

_____

_____

_____

12. What one thing could be done that would help your family immensely?

_____

_____

_____

A more serious dream...

When I write down my dreams, I put down a lot of fun, exotic and crazy things. I would go to Hawaii, Europe, Alaska and I would take many cruises. There is nothing wrong with this type of dreaming. Write them down and pursue them. They can come true for you. But at some point you will have traveled all you wish, you will have a good handle on your money and you will begin to ask the question again, "is that all there is?"

This is a place where many people have what is called an existential crisis. Existential crisis is a fancy word that simply means, "Why am I here?" What is the meaning of my existence on this earth? All of us hit this wall at different times in our lives wondering why we are here and is what I'm doing the right thing for me?

I hit this wall hard when I went to college. After the first round of tests, I realized I could handle college. I could pass all of my courses and in four years I would graduate with a degree in psychology. The question came to me, so? So I stay in college 4 years and graduate - then what? Well, I go to work for 30 years and retire, so? Is that all there is? Is this what I want with my life? You may recall hitting this wall at different times in your life. Many people hit this wall when they graduate from high school or college. Some hit it right after they marry. Most of us feel it every 7 years which the old timers called the 7-year itch. Some people never put it into words, but they certainly feel it on their 30th, 40th or 50th birthdays. What is the meaning of life and why am I here?

When these questions came to me during my freshman year in college, I could not move. I couldn't study, I couldn't concentrate, and I couldn't date. I really had to sit down and work on this question. So I began to research this question, "Why are were here?"

I found some remarkable things. The first thing I found is that philosophers, ministers, politicians, teachers have been studying this question for centuries. Second, I discovered they had found some answers. Let's look at a few of them.

First, some people believe we are here simply to learn. This is big among new age thinkers today. We are each born here with something to learn, and we must keep working till we learn what it is we are sent here to learn. But there must be more to life than simply learning.

What I have found is there is a great deal of meaning in life by becoming the best you can be. If you will simply turn this idea around and strive to be the best you can be, you will move past mere learning and more into personal growth. This is one of the reasons we are here.

Second, some people see life as nothing more than one big party with the motto "Eat drink and be merry for tomorrow we may die." There is a modern day expression that says, "Life is short, eat dessert first." Well, this turns life into a very self-centered existence and it can be extremely destructive. There is more to life than "party at all costs."

What I have found is there is a sense in which life is a gift from God and the best way to say thank you for a gift is to enjoy that gift to its fullest. So having fun and doing those things you love is part of why we are here.

Third, some secular people take a very crass look at life and conclude we are like any other animal and the only reason we are here is to perpetuate the species. This seems a little crazed to me. Having children just so we can have children for the sole reason to keep life going seems a little futile.

There is value and meaning in life for those of us fortunate enough to have children, teach them value and goodness and then see them succeed. Connection to family, both historic and future, is **one** of the reasons we are here, but it is not the **only** reason.

Fourth, some people find meaning in life by helping others. It is very true that helping a person find their way can be very valuable. Contributing to the betterment of people is extremely satisfying and can provide a great deal of meaning to life. Teachers, nurses, politicians, ministers, Boy Scout leaders, volunteers, philanthropists and even business managers can attest to this.

However, there is a danger here we must be careful to avoid. Some philosophies teach that helping others is the only reason people are here and they run into real problems with their people becoming martyrs for others with the hope of rewards after this life. You can see this in a family that has one person who gives and gives and gives but will accept nothing, not even gratitude, in return.

Fifth. One evening well after dark, I took a seat underneath a tree where I sat and pondered this research for over 2 hours. This is where I came up with the answer to the meaning of life for me. My conclusion is that God wanted someone to love and He created us so He could have someone to love. I can find meaning to my life by loving God. This was a great revelation for me. I got up from my tree and was able to go back to class and complete my education, because I could love God by being my best, loving others and connecting with my family. This revelation gave direction to my life for years to come.

The message I need to make very clear in this section of the book is **you can deepen your life, you can create more value, meaning and quality to your life by developing dreams in each of these 5 areas.** What dreams do you need to develop in the areas of personal growth? What dreams do you need to develop in the areas of enjoying life more? What dreams do you need to develop in the areas of family, helping others and spirituality?

1. Personal Growth

In the end we are all seeking happiness. What will then make you happy? Social psychologist David G. Myers Ph.D. has written in his book, "The Pursuit of Happiness," that money, age, race, sex and education have little to do with how happy we feel. What matters more are self-esteem, involvement with others, an outgoing personality, a sense of hope and work we enjoy. It is possible to set dreams and goals for each of these areas of life as well.

Self-Esteem: Self-esteem is feeling good about yourself. It is knowing you can accomplish what you want to accomplish. What 3 things can you do this week that will increase your self esteem?

_____

_____

_____

Outgoing Personality: Developing your personality is possible also. Memorizing jokes, reading and seeing movies helps to make your conversations more interesting. There is an old adage, "If you want a friend, be a friend." What can you do to improve your personality...

_____

_____

_____

Fostering a sense of hope is also important to happiness. You can set goals in this area also. Life gives us a sense of hope with the birth of a new baby and the budding of spring. What gives you hope?

_____

_____

_____

Do you need to improve in the area of time management?

_____

_____

_____

Do you need to improve in the area of your health?

_____

_____

_____

2. Enjoying Life More

If happiness is what we are all seeking, what would make you happier? Write 3 dreams here.

_____

_____

_____

3. Connection to Family and Friends

The first connection here should be in the areas of family and relatives. But developing more significant relationships with friends is possible also. If you are like me, you have a number of two-minute relationships where you meet someone in the hall of your work and you speak for two minutes exchanging business ideas and maybe a "how are you." It is possible to create deeper relationships, but it does take time.

My wife and I were wanting some deeper friendships, so we made a list of 5 couples we wanted to get to know better. We invited them out to dinner then over for a cookout and slowly we were able to grow some deeper friendships.

Perhaps you would like to make such a list, or join a professional association or a charity group to help people. There are dreams you can imagine in this area.

_____

_____

_____

4. Helping Others

In what ways can you plant trees under which you will never sit? Girl Scouts, Boy Scouts, Little league...

_____

_____

_____

5. Spiritual Life

You can set spiritual goals as well as personal goals.

_____

_____

_____

Find the "Why" behind each dream.
Why dream!

While speaking in Nashville recently, a young man approached me and said, "I sold my business recently and I really don't know what to do next. I don't have any dreams." This young man, who looked to be about 45, could dream, but he had not found reasons to dream. Sometimes we need to start with arbitrary dreams they will help us get back to the dreaming process, but life will be limited unless we find some meaningful reasons to dream. We must connected a "why" to their dreams. We must connect an emotional reason to our dreams, that will compel the completion of the dream. Let's look at some standard reasons for dreaming.

1. Dreams determine our future.

Would you rather live a life that is designed by you or a life that is given to you by other people and the circumstances of this world? Dreams can help you determine your future.

You can take whatever job the company offers you or you can dream of the perfect job within the company and develop your skills and relationships to get that job. Which way would be better for you and your family and the company? The dreaming way of course. You will be more productive in a job you like. You will improve because of the extra education you seek, and because we are usually good at what we like to do, you will no doubt be paid more.

Many people live in the area of town their parents lived in or that is close to their work. They choose the neighborhood based on what they think they can best afford. Dreamers, on the other hand, look at the entire city and determine the best area for their family, work and lifestyle and they begin working for that end. They let their dreams determine their future and where they will live not just the current constrains of their pocket book.

You can live in your current house or apartment for the rest of your life or you can dream of the perfect home for you. Maybe you want a very simple home for sleeping and an occasional meal. Maybe you dream of an elegant home designed especially for rest and replenishing your soul with soft jazz and a warm fire. Maybe you dream of an artistic home near theaters, restaurants and galleries. Maybe you dream of a home in the country or on a mountain.

Maybe you dream of a fit body or a money-making hobby or a trip to Hawaii. Whatever your dream, your future will be determined by the dreams you dream. With no dreams, your future will be determined by accident. With dreams, you can design your future.

I love the quote by Earl Nightingale. "The world will turn aside and let a person pass who knows where he or she is going."

2. Dreams can destroy reality.

I love the phrase that says, "If reality can destroy dreams, then dreams can destroy reality." I know people and you do too who are facing extremely difficult circumstances. When you are facing an abusive spouse, a terrible disease or financial strain, it's hard. "What do I do?" is the desperate cry we all understand. The one thing I do know is dreaming of a better future and moving toward that dream can destroy your reality.

The best example of this is a young lady by the name of Carole Smith. She was facing a terrible disease called Multiple Sclerosis (MS). It is a disease that is big enough to consume every thought and waking moment of your life. Carole picked up a copy of my first book, "Follow Your Dreams," and began to read and dream. She would spend time in the evening reading the book and designing her future.

Carole's dream of opening an art gallery became bigger than her circumstances. Today the LionHeart gallery in Louisville Kentucky conducts classes in creativity, sells sculptures, paintings and photographs and specializes in Kentucky artists. Way to go, Carole! You're allowing your dreams instead of your circumstances to control your life.

3. Dreams give us a reason to live.

Humans were created to be goal seeking. As infants we seek food, warmth and rest. As children we seek love, friendship and attention. As adults we need new stimulating goals to keep us moving, learning and growing. Dreams provide this reason to live.

Even if your dream is simple, it gives you a reason to get up in the morning and move forward. Maybe your dream is simply to pay your bills and stay healthy. This is still good enough to get you up in the morning and to a job.

Yet stop to think how much more excitement and joy there would be in your life if you had a dream of helping other people through your work, church and family. How much more compelling would your life be if your goal was to create a $1,000,000 estate to leave to your family or a college?

Dreams provide the reason to get out of bed, go to work and create art, business, friendships and estates. If you are stagnated in your personal life or professional life, if you are bored with your present state, check out your dreams. Is it time to dream higher?

4. Dreams are fun.

Dreams can provide some of the richest joy in your life. Dreams can be pure fun. A friend of mine and I recently took a trip to Lookout Mountain Tennessee to hang glide. We drove down on a Friday, got up early the next morning and set out to hang glide. They strap you to a wing made of nylon as thin as paper and held together with plastic pipe. You are strapped in and told to hang on to the instructor. A plane pulls you up, then the rope is cut and you're set free. I was reminded of the song in the 60's, "bankin' off of the northeast wind, sailin' on a summer breeze, skippin' over the ocean like a stone." It was stupid and crazy and just pure fun.

Traveling to Europe, Russia and Japan has provided some of the best growing experiences of my life. I have learned about myself, about other people and experienced things I could never experience in Kentucky. Dreams provided that enjoyment.

How much fun would it be if you and your spouse set a dream of visiting every state park or every winery in your state? I knew a minister once who had taken his family camping in 20 different states. This was a favorite activity and a great bonding time with his family. What a dream! Take time to dream something strictly for fun.

Assignment: For every dream you wrote down go back and write why you want to accomplish this dream. It is the "why" that will make your dream come true.

Section II

"What is Stopping You?"

"Find those things that stop you from being successful and one by one eliminate them and you will be successful!"

Bobby Knight

Step 4
Find What is Stopping You!

It is hard to study success very long without taking a long look a failure. As Les Brown says, "failure is a part of the success process." As much as we want to succeed, we must look at those things stopping us from accomplishing our dreams.

Take a moment and list all the things stopping you. List those obvious things such as children, physical limitations and bad habits. Also list those subtle things you may not think about all the time. Do you have a bad attitude about money? Do you see yourself as a failure and therefore expect to fail in everything you set out to do? Do you feel exhausted at everything you have to do and therefore cannot consider any new activity? List your limitations.

1.
2.
3.
4.
5.
6.

In the next 3 chapters, let us explore some ideas you may not have thought about.

"Great sprits have always found
violent opposition from mediocre minds."
Albert Einstein

External Pressures

The Nibblers

Have you met the nibblers? Those people and things that take tiny bits out of your idea or motivation? **Beware of the nibblers they can kill your dreams!**

Have you ever taken a great idea to a committee? One person will disagree with the idea and it loses a little power. Another person will make a slight modification to your suggestion that makes it a little smaller. Then the flood gates open and an entire rush of suggestions and modifications start being attached to your idea. Pretty soon your great idea is nibbled down to an average idea. This same process can happen with your dreams. When you take your dream to a group of people who have very small dreams themselves, they don't like the fact that your dreams are bigger than theirs. They want you to be at a similar size as they are. So they gather around you and one takes a bite and another takes a bite and a third until your dream is the same size as theirs.

Suppose you have a dream of becoming a pilot. Wow! That is a big challenging dream. So you go and tell your mother your exciting news. She responds "Oh, no. That's so dangerous." Now no one wants to hurt their own mother, so you think maybe I should not become a pilot. She, in a sincere concern for your safety, has taken the first nibble out of your dream.

After a couple of days you mention this dream to your father, whom you know has always been financially astute. He says, "Man, do you know how much it costs to become a pilot, rent an airplane and buy fuel and insurance? Son, it will cost you $2,500 a year just to maintain your plane and license. If you put $2,500 a year for 5 years in the bank, you will have $12,500 plus interest. You could send your son to a year of college with that kind of money." Well, no one wants to be stupid with their money and the way your father speaks makes it sure sound stupid to spend $2,500 a year for a hobby. And who would not want to send their kid to college?

Your father has just taken a second bite out of your big dream.

Then you mention it to a friend, who tells you your'e not smart enough to become a pilot. Then someone pipes up with a brilliant statement like "90% of people who fly get so airsick they can't fly in hot weather." Boom. The third and fourth bites of your dream are gone.

If these people thought being a pilot was a good idea, they would have gone and done it themselves. So when you bring your dream to them, they feel obligated to tell you why they are not doing that idea. They unknowingly keep cutting down your dream until itís the same size as theirs, which many times is no dream at all!

I have a new motto in life, "Kill the good-for-nothing nibblers!"

>Kill the nibblers!
>Kill the nibblers!
>Kill the nibblers!

Another quick example. Suppose you set a dream to earn $250,000 a year selling real estate. Oh, the nibblers will come out. Nibbler #1 says "The average real estate salesman earns $18,500 a year. You will have to sell 13 times more than the average sales person to earn $250,000. I know you are above average, but are you 13 times above average?" Nibbler #2 says, "Oh, that no money down stuff is a rip off." Nibbler #3 says, "Man, the real estate field is so competitive, 90% of the new hires wash out in the first year." Nibbler #4 says, "Oh, I tried real estate once and lost my shirt."Another nibbler might say, "Didn't you hear they are doing away with the tax incentives for investment real estate?"

After the nibblers comment on your dream you walk away saying, "Oh gee, did I make the right decision?" And you might have a tendency to lower your dream to the same size as the rest of these nibblers.

Let me ask a question. Does it make sense to get advice on a real estate career from people who have never sold real estate? Or worse yet, does it make sense to get advice about your real estate

career from people who have tried real estate and failed? NO!

Once I had a prominent CPA tell me he had bought two pieces of property and lost money on them and sold them just so he could tell people that real estate was not a good investment. To which I retorted, "Would you go to a CPA who had only done two tax returns and failed at both of them?" "No," he agreed, "I would seek out a competent CPA."

The same is true of your dreams. Don't hang around the nay sayers and the failures in your field. Kill the nibblers and seek out those who have been successful in your field. Go to the rallies, conventions and association meetings where the winners in your field hang out. Read the books, take the classes and learn from the best in your field. This will make your dreams bigger and keep the nibblers at bay.

The Cynics

It's amazing the number of great ideas and dreams killed by the laughter of a family member, colleague, or expert. When you tell someone about an idea you have, often you will hear a soft chuckle or a silent turn away from them. This soft but distinct rebuff to your idea has killed many a good dream. Many times the so-called expert has thought of the idea themselves and never done anything about it, or they have seen others try a similar idea and fail. If they thought it was a good idea, they would be doing it themselves. Since they are not doing it obviously it's not a good idea.

This is a disease known as cynicism. It can be found in people of any age, any ethnic background and any education level. It often happens to people who have tried a few things and failed and to people who think they've seen it all. According to Webster's, cynicism is a belief that people are motivated in all their actions only by selfishness. It denies the sincerity of people's actions or of the value of living.

You can tell cynics by the sentences they use. "Oh, that won't work" is often spoken by a cynic before they have heard the entire idea. "We've tried that before and it didn't work and it won't work now." "We've never done it that way before." You will find among educated people a subtle belief that cynicism is the highest form of the intellectual humor. They take great delight in putting down people and ideas with humorous twists on words.

There are three things to say about cynics. First, the cynic is always right. There is a sense in which people do act out of self interest, but thatís not the final word on people. We are so much more than cynicism provides. Second, the cynic enjoys laughing at people and life; therefore, they always have a subject. Third, at the end of the day, **THE CYNIC NEVER HELPS US!** The cynic does not help us, our dreams or the world in general. So, why do we listen to them?

If you find yourself around a bunch of cynics, RUN LIKE A BIG DOG! Dreaming a new thing and working to make it come true is the highest form of the intellect and the highest use of the abilities God has given us. You deserve better. Find yourself a group of young hungry people who still believe things are possible and hang around them.

Circumstances

Many of us find ourselves in circumstances that hinder our dreams. These external circumstances may be the job we have, the type of career we have chosen, the family we were born into, the friends we hang around or poor financial circumstances. It is very easy to view external circumstances as things beyond our control. And of course, some of them are truly beyond our control. If a truck hits you and breaks your leg that, of course, is an external circum-stance beyond your control. But many of us take this too far. We start viewing everything that happens to us as beyond our control.

Sociologists have referred to this as the locus of control. Do you see the locus of control as being outside of you or do you see the locus of control as inside you? If you see the locus of control as outside you, you feel everything that happens to you is from the outside, and you feel you don't have any control. It is easy for this person to blame every good and bad thing in their life as "God's will" or on the winds of fate. This type of attitude will always slow you down.

If you see the locus of control as inside you, you see life as full of possibilities and you have some control, even a great deal of control in how these possibilities will turn out. You feel much more in control. This view of life provides a great deal of hope and can be very inspiring.

I have found it extremely helpful to look at all my circumstances as something I can control. When I see my health, my friends and the way I am treated as something I can control, my attitude is better, my sense of hope is better and my motivation to do things is better. Maybe you have heard the old adage, "We make our own luck." This is the attitude I now attack the world with.

This type of attitude is far more realistic than it is fantasy. Some people, of course, are struck with cancer or some other terrible disease by heredity, but most of us have bad health because of bad health habits. We love fried food instead of vegetables causing our bad health. Most of us have money problems because we spend more money than we bring in or we do not save for those bad situations that arise. Many people get caught up in smoking or drugs or bad situations because of the people they hang around. You see, many of the circumstances in our life are in our control.

I have an uncle in Arkansas by the name of Buford Stone (we call him uncle BS). Uncle BS has smoked 2 packs of cigarettes a day for 45 years. The only exercise he gets is walking to the mail box or pushing the remote on his TV. For 45 years he has eaten fried sausage, eggs and hash browns for breakfast, fried hamburgers for lunch and fried chicken, mashed potatoes and milk gravy for dinner. Now at age 51, he has heart problems. And he wants me to feel sorry for him.

BULLFEATHERS!!!...that's a euphemism!
My uncle has made his own circumstances. He is the one who has smoked for 45 years. He is the one who has chosen to eat fried meat, donuts and french fries 3 times a day for 45 years. His heart problem is not because of his parents or the outside world but because of his own choices.

Whatever circumstances you currently face, write them down. Think about whether the circumstances are actually outside you or did you create the circumstances you face? If they are truly from outside you, do you still have some control over them? The answer is probably yes yes yes.

"Knowing your own darkness is the best method for dealing with the darkness of other people."
Carl Jung

Past

The past is something that seems to stop so many people. One thing is for sure -- **you will never move forward until you deal with your past.**

There are three types of problems with our past. First, you inherited a problem. Many people who were born into an ethnic group or short or overweight or with a disease, face this problem with their past of feeling they were born unlucky. Second, you may have had difficulties with your parents. People who were born into families of alcoholics or abusive parents, deal constantly with their past. Third, you have made poor choices. This is often the lament of people who married too young or got into trouble with the law or didn't go to college.

When I was a little boy around 6 years of age, my mother told my sister and I at the dinner table she preferred to use the small fork when she ate. To her this fork was more dainty and therefore more ladylike. For some reason that conversation emotionally struck a chord with me and it changed my preferences. To this day I prefer eating with a salad fork. On another occasion, our family sat down to eat and we began to pass the fried chicken around. My mother, sensing dad had had a rough day and wanting him to feel special, said to my sister and me, "Let dad have the first piece of chicken. Let him have that big breast of the chicken." I was so envious of dad getting the biggest piece of chicken. He also got what our family considered the best piece of chicken. I know this is stupid, but to this day I still prefer white meat and choose the breast of chicken if I have a choice. I, of course, eat it as well as my entire meal with my salad fork. HeHe!!

This really scares me. If something as simple as preferences for forks and chicken can be determined by a casual comment of my mother, what else has been determined in my life by the casual comments of my parents or someone else I admire? Do you vote democratic because your parents or family did? Do you live from paycheck to paycheck no matter how much money you make because this is the way your family lived? Do you work 60 hours a week because you saw your father or mother working that much? Or maybe your family didn't work that much, but you donít want to live in poverty and therefore you work 60 hours a week. What types of things are you doing today because of the emotional baggage you picked up during your childhood?

How much more was your life altered if you experienced a rape or a bankruptcy or a loss of a family member to AIDS? You see many of our actions can be based on problems we encountered in our past. And we will never be as successful as we can be if we do not first deal with our past.

If we simply ignore our past, we are doomed to live out in adulthood the problems we picked up in the past. This is seen in someone born into an abusive home. If they do not deal with the problems of being abused, often they will grow up to be abusers themselves. The same is true with bad spending habits, alcoholism, and other problems. Have you ever caught yourself saying something to your kids you remember hearing your parents say that you swore you would never say? The only answer is to break the cycle. Here are 4 steps for getting control of your past and moving on toward your dreams.

1. Identify the problem. Many problems we face are never named and therefore remain vague and unknown. The best way to name the problem is to write it down in clear simple terms. "My parents seemed to struggle with money all their lives. Perhaps this is why I still struggle with money." This is a clear expression of naming the problem.

2. Write down every detail of the problem. There are usually thousands of angles from which this problem may affect you. Write them all down. If your parents struggled with money, then this affects your spending habits today. It may also affect how much you eat or how cheap you are on a date.

Also try to write down any scenario that is ingrained in your memory. A good story about your family or emotional situation that describes your feelings about your problem of the past can be very insightful. You can learn volumes by the stories you tell.

2a. If you can trace how far back this problem goes in your family, you may find the same problem was faced by members of your family for 6 generations. This may help explain how you received this problem and it may alert you to how you are passing it on to your children.

2b. Identify a particular behavior you are engaging in because of the difficulties you have had in the past. If one of your parents drank, maybe you find yourself not feeling alive unless there is intense chaos in your life. Children of alcoholic parents often create problems in their own lives even if the problems donít really exist.

3. Embrace the truth about yourself. You are a person created by God. You have a problem with your past. Thatís OK. God loves you problems and all. Envision the arms of a good friend or of your mother or of God reaching around you to embrace you. They do not ask if you are perfect, they simply love you as you are. This is what you must do with yourself. Embrace the whole person warts and all and say, "I am good." If someone treated you badly as a child, it's OK to admit it. You did not do the bad thing, someone else did. Even if you did do something terrible, that does not define all of who you are. You are more than the problems of your past.

4. Find a way to reframe the problem. You may need to get some professional help if you are facing a serious emotional wound. But in the end you need to find a way to say to yourself, "The problem I faced is in the past. It was helpful to me in some ways and it was destructive in some ways. But today I am through with this problem. It will control my life no more."

5. Write a single statement describing the new behavior you want to live. This we call an affirmation. Read this sentence twice a day. You will be amazed how much this helps.

6. Begin to act with your new behavior. It will be hard at first, but if you can act on the new behavior for 21 days, you will begin to create a new habit.

"*Inside each of us are thoughts
and beliefs that hinder our
dreams from coming true.*"
Conway Stone

Internal Pressures

1. We Build our Own Prisons

Sitting on the tailgate of an old red pickup truck near Crooked Creek Kentucky, an old navy man was talking to my father and three men of the neighborhood. One man piped up and said he was going to buy a farm tractor and bushhog so he could do some mowing for different farms around the county. The old navy guy replied, "Oh, you're going to buy yourself a job."

"No!" the man replied quickly. "Well, I guess I am. I never thought of it that way. Man, I've already got a job. I don't want to buy another one."

"We build our own prisons," responded the old navy man. "If you buy that tractor you would have built a prison wall of the debt. That's OK. All of us can handle one wall, but without thinking about it you have built another prison wall of debt because you'll have ongoing maintenance of the tractor (repairs, gas, tires, etc.). And if two walls don't hold you, when you sign contracts to mow farms, you will have built another prison wall regarding your time. Pretty soon you have built a serious prison in which you have to live."

I saw all three men nod in agreement. The man did not buy the tractor.

How many prisons have we built for ourselves? How many of us have built financial prisons because we bought more than we could afford? How many of us have built labor camps for ourselves because we have chosen professions offering few opportunities for advancement? How many of us have created prisons for ourselves because we have beliefs that are killing our talents and potential?

I remember my mother saying to me as I grew up, "Conway, you are just like me. I can't spell and you can't either." Because my mother believed this, she would repeat this statement and chuckle slightly every time I struggled with the spelling of a word. She would cut me some slack when it came time for spelling quizzes and even the final spelling grade in school. The problem is I bought into this belief. This belief became a prison I built in my own mind. When anyone would ask me how to spell a word, my first answer was, "I can't spell." This got me off the hook. But because of this prison, I struggled in high school, college and graduate school.

As I got older, I realized I was as smart as anyone else and I could learn to spell. So I began to tear that prison wall down. It went slow at first. I had to begin one brick at a time. I decided I could spell - one big brick gone. I began to read books on spelling and two, three and four bricks were gone.

For those of you who want to know, the scientific and psychological theory behind this idea can be found in a book written by Dr. Martin Seligman. Dr. Seligman wrote a book[2] entitled "Helplessness" in which he describes learned helplessness. (Oh yes, required reading in graduate school.) His concept simply says in several ways, both obvious and subtle, we teach ourselves to be helpless. Let's explore a couple of attitudes we hold in our minds forming prisons blocking our success.

> I'm poor but happy... why not be rich and happy?
> I'm just that way... why not be another way?
> Better safe than sorry... why not be safe & happy?
> Love is blind... Does it have to be? Is this an excuse we're giving ourselves?
> I earn $30,000 a year... Oh really. Why not $130,000 a year?

What beliefs or actions have you chosen that have built prison walls for you to live in? A young girl who decides to get pregnant at 16 will live with the child until she is 36 years of age. A person who eats donuts and French fries every day for 30 years will create a prison of his/her own weight. A person who spends more money than they make will one day live in a serious financial prison. The good news is you can get out of prisons you build for yourself.

---

[2]"Helplessness" by Martin E. P. Seligman Published 1975.

One final story to illustrate this point. A story is told of the great illusionist Harry Houdini who made a living escaping from death defying traps. Many times he would get publicity for his shows by escaping from the local jails. One day an old prison guard from south Georgia challenged Houdini by saying he could not escape from his dinky Mayberry RFD type prison. Taking the challenge, Houdini was locked in the cell. Houdini, who had been accustomed to breaking out of a cell within 8 to 10 minutes, began to work. He worked an hour, then two, then four, then 8 hours. He continued to work through the night and after 18 hours, he fell down with exhaustion. When falling he fell against the jail cell door and the door swung freely open. The door had never been locked. The cell was locked only in Houdini's mind, but that's all that was needed. It was locked as securely as if it had been locked with 50 chains.

If we have beliefs in our minds that are limiting our growth, it doesn't matter if the beliefs are true. They will limit us anyway.

2. We Dream But We Don't Mean It!

There is an ancient scripture that says, "You have not because you ask not, and when you ask you ask amiss." What this phrase is trying to say, is when we ask, we ask without caring, without really meaning it. We ask crazily. Have you ever heard someone say, "I'd like to be a millionaire."? But you know they have a $25,000 a year job and no plan for earning their million dollars.

I call this wishful thinking. It is more fantasy or wishing than it is serious dreaming. It is dreaming without care. In order to accomplish our dreams we must move from fantasy to follow a serious dream process. The question I ask people to test whether they're serious about their dreams is, "Are you willing to exchange your time, energy and money for that dream?" Life is simply made up of time and energy. Are you willing to exchange your time and energy to see that dream fulfilled? This is dreaming for real.

3. Romanticized Dreams

When I went to college, I dreamed of becoming a psychologist. I had this picture in my head of what a psychologist was. I pictured myself sitting at an oak desk surrounded by piles and piles of books nodding my head slightly as people told me about their lives. When they finished, I would throw out a couple of quotes and watch the light bulbs come on as they went out that day and changed their lives.

Do you know any psychologist living such a life? I can tell you for sure no psychologist is living this way. The work of a psychologist is hard, tenuous, competitive and filled with hurting and difficult people. I thank God everyday I do not live such a life. I had a romantic ideal of what a psychologist was which propelled a dream that was not right for me.

When people learn I'm an author, they often tell me they want to become a writer. When I probe deeper, they tell me romantic dreams of sitting in Hawaii writing on their laptop as ocean waves lap around their feet. A beautiful young lady brings them a phone call from their agent who tells them their great American novel has just hit the best seller list. Being an author with a fair amount of success, I can tell you the life of a writer is far less romantic than this.

One of the things that kills people is they are following romantic dreams rather than real life dreams. The dream must be real and it must be something you want to do because it's worthy of your life.

4. We Don't Believe We can Achieve Our Dreams

Do you believe you can achieve the dream or do you catch yourself saying, "I'd like to do this, but I don't really believe I can."? Accomplishing a dream with this attitude is extremely difficult.

Sometimes I like to define motivation as "believing it is possible." If you believe something is possible, most of the time you are motivated to do it. Nothing is more deflating or unmotivating than believing something is not possible.

After years of research we have found that people act based on what they believe. If you believe a seminar is good for you, you will go. If you believe the seminar is not particularly good, you'll stay home.

Can you see how this connects with your dream? If you believe in your heart the dream can be done, your chances of accomplishing the dream are much better.

What are the belief systems stopping you? List them out. Then one by one find a solution to that problem. Like a gardener weeds the garden, so we must weed our lives of the things that distract us from accomplishing our dreams.

1. doubts
2. boredom
3. lack of energy
4. too busy
5. negative attackers
6. road blocks
7. money problems
8. people say no
9. people let you down
10. your priorities change
11. Nibblers

Here is a step-by-step process that will help you weed out the distractions...

1. Write them down. Most people ignore their weaknesses and therefore never deal with them. This kind of denial can derail your success process. Acknowledging the problems is the first step to eliminating them.

Ask one of your closest friends if they can tell you some of the difficulties they see in your life. It's difficult to be so vulnerable, but this is a very profitable exercise.

Sometime when you are doing some boring work such as stuffing envelopes or taking a long car ride, begin to think about the things hindering you from moving forward. With a blank pad write down every idea that comes to your mind. This can be very surprising. With this exercise I once filled up 5 legal size pages of things that were stopping me.

2. Analyze why you have those problems in your life. If you are always behind in your finances, is it because you don't make enough money or your spending habits are bad or you grew up with bad money habits and you are living out that same lifestyle today?

You may find this exercise difficult but stay with it. It is very important to understand why you have a certain problem in your life.

3. Develop a plan around each problem. One by one devise a plan around each problem. You may need some help if you are facing problems that seem bigger than you. A counselor, minister or sales manager can be very helpful.

4. Believe you can overcome the problem. The old adage "Hope springs eternal in the human breast" is true, but some of us have to work at it. Know that whatever the problem, you can overcome it. Without this hope most people simply give up.

5. Work your plan. Have you heard the old adage, "Plan your work and work your plan."? Yes, it all boils down to work. Pat Summitt in her book, "Reach for the Summit," about being the head coach of Tennessee women's basketball says, "No matter how good you are, I will simply out-work you." She states this as one of her success secrets. That is a secret we can use. When following your dreams, work hard on yourself, your own habits, and on understanding your weakness. This may be the hardest work you will ever do, but this is where you can gain real advantage over others and over those things that are stopping your progress. Bobby Knight says, "If you want to be successful, find those things stopping you and one by one eliminate them, and you will be successful."

6. Find a role model. Whatever problem you find that may be stopping you, find a role model of people who have accomplished their dreams even though they have faced the same problems you have. I love to collect inspiring stories of people who have accomplished their dreams. I want to share a couple of these inspiring stories with you, based around some of the common excuses we all hear.

I'm too poor to follow my dreams.

Oseola McCarty spent a lifetime washing people's clothes. Day after day for almost 87 years, she charged $10.00 for a bundle of dirty clothes and made them clean and neat for people in her home town of Hattiesburg Mississippi. She is a descendant of slaves and having never had the opportunity for formal education, she wanted to do something for the young people of her city. But what could she do? Dream High! That's what.

She began to save. Of course it was small and almost stupid - one dollar then ten dollars then 100 dollars. But what is this compared to the price of a college education these days? Some dreams start small, some even start with a dollar. Over the years she amassed a savings of $150,000. She donated the entire amount to the University of Southern Mississippi to help young people go to college!

In Mrs. McCarty's words, "My only real regret is that I never went to school. I hope these children will not have to work as I did and will be able to go to school." Stephanie Bullock an 18-year-old honor student in high school was the first to receive a scholarship. The $1,000 scholarship covered half of her tuition.

No, being poor is no excuse. We can all accomplish great dreams.

I face serious prejudice, I'm the wrong color.

Since I am not a person of color, it is hard for me to address this issue. I would like to offer the following ideas as a word of hope for the people of color who are reading this book. Ms. McCarty in the above scenario is an African American woman. The Census Bureau reported that African American owned businesses have increased 46% in recent years. The profits from those businesses have grown to $32 billion annually. The census bureau goes on to state that more and more African Americans are retiring younger, and going on to start their own businesses.

Despite hardships they dreamed of opening an art gallery! Today the Lionheart Gallery is a reality.

Carole & Gary Smith, dreamers.

We do have a lot of problems in this country, but this place is still a land of opportunity even for people of color.

I'm too old.

Mrs. Johnnie Jones announced her intention to return to college at age 75. "What are you going to do with the degree?" her family asked. "I'm going to put that degree on the wall and salute it every day." That was 9 years ago. Today at age 84, Mrs. Jones has graduated from the University of Louisville with honors. She did not let race, gender or age get in her way.

Have you ever heard of "ram jet ventilation?" It's a term to refer to the type of breathing sharks do. Sharks don't have lungs and muscles that expand and contract so they can breathe. Instead they have 507 gills that allow water to pass through their bodies. The trick is they must keep moving so that water is forced through their gills and thus into their bodies. If they stop moving, they die. (Don't ask me how they sleep.)

We as people are that way. We must keep moving or we die as well. Stop moving, start complaining, retire to a rocking chair or stop dreaming and your body atrophies and you turn from muscle to fat. Your mind atrophies as well. It moves from sharp to dull and your spirit grows cold and cynical. The message is simple - **dream or die.**

With dreams and goals, we can keep ourselves moving and growing much longer than we ever thought possible. Marie Wilcox-Little is a great example. She is a daily swimmer at age 73. Roy Erlandson began competitive swimming at age 60 and still swims at age 82.

Marian Haas Anderson enjoys snow skiing at age 74. Her comments on her age, "Each day to me is a new adventure, unrelated to what has gone before or what will follow. I am optimistic about my capabilities and intolerant of the limitations my bones would impose. Life for the most part has been very good to me, but if I had it to do over again I would do it entirely differently just for fun."

What an attitude! Yes, you can do many things no matter how

old you are. Too old? **NEVER!**

I love the story of the Marin Rowing Association that enjoys rowing for fun as a sport. The average age of the members is 76.

MARIN ROWING ASSOCIATION
(average age 76 years young)

Wales

Rafting in Provence, France

I'm too young.

This one seems so petty, I almost hate to cover it, but some people do feel their age is a hindrance. Let's state clearly some of the best accomplishments in our history achieved by young people. Martin Luther King Jr. was just 26 when he led the boycott in Montgomery Alabama. Debbie Fields was just 20 years of age when she started Mrs. Fields Cookies. Macaulay Culkin was a very young 10 years of age when he made "Home Alone" in 1990. In 1992 & 1993 he earned $23,000,000.

But my favorite example is of Larry Villa who at age 11 invented a sprinkler that will water a tree and nothing else. This simple circular plastic device anyone could have thought of, but it took an 11 year old kid to do it. His invention grossed $70,000 in 1994. Don't let your age stop you. Dream and achieve anyway.

I'm stuck in bad circumstances.

This excuse is also very tempting on the surface. There are many people who were born into an ethnic group or crippled or find themselves fighting a debilitating disease. Still others fight bad circumstances such as a bad marriage, dead-end jobs or bad financial situations. Admitting the bad situation you are facing is good and healthy. Throwing your hands up and quitting because of your situation is not.

Some of the bad circumstances we face are our own doing. Addiction, poor spending habits, bad health because of bad eating habits. History is replete with examples of people who have overcome bad situations to achieve greatness. Abraham Lincoln overcame poverty and many losing campaigns. Sam Walton went bankrupt 2 times before working his magic with Wal-Mart. You can overcome the prison walls you create. It takes a while but changing the decisions you make can eventually change the situations.

History is also replete with stories of triumph of people who have been born into bad circumstances. Franklin Delano Roosevelt contracted polio but went on to become President of the United States. Andrew Young faced hardship but went on to work with Dr. King and to be Ambassador to the United Nations. Helen Keller, born blind and deaf, went on to become a profound writer, speaker and example. You can overcome your circumstances.

WHAT MOTIVATES ME?

RANK: #1=Most motivating to #21= least motivating

___ enjoyment/fun	___ physical health	___ sex
___ family and/or friendship	___ power	___ self preservation
___ independence	___ professional achievements	___ freedom of body & mind
___ material objects	___ security	___ revenge
___ mental health	___ status	___ fear
___ money in the bank	___ love	___ self-expression & recognition
___ personal achievements	___ material gain	___ life after death

Charlie Gatton dreamer and engineer

At age 75 he still climbs the roof to help others. Charlie is a crew chief for Habitat.

The Heroes Club sponsors three
Habitat for Humanity Houses.

"The absurd man is he who never changes."
Auguste Barthelemy

What is Stopping You?

Of all the things that get in the way of our dreams and stop us from being all that God intended for us to be, whether it be age, health, circumstances, family, our past or our beliefs, is there anything we cannot overcome? A spiritual friend of mine suggested we have different voices inside us. One voice may be negative saying, "I can't." Another voice may be a voice of inferiority saying, "I'm not good enough." Another voice may say, "I'm too busy."

Still there are voices inside us saying, "I wonder if I could do this?" There are dreamer voices saying, "I wish I could travel to…" The truth is we can choose to listen to any of the voices we wish. We can let the negative ones subside and we can choose to listen to the positive ones.

We must be reminded that any problem we face we can overcome. We live in a place and a time in history in which we can overcome the most devastating problems and succeed. While attending a conference in Chicago, a man came up and spoke to me about his time in America. He had stood on the wall with Lech Walensa in Poland. But when the democracy movement waned, he was forced to flee and came to America. Later his wife joined him here, but after a year of separation and all that went on, it was difficult to stay together and they divorced. Leaving his country and losing his family, he paid dearly for his stand for freedom. Today, however, he is a professional financial planner and enjoys his life in Chicago. If he can overcome political exile, you and I can overcome our obstacles.

I met another young man in Indianapolis Indiana recently who told me he had moved there from Switzerland. I was aghast! How could anyone leave Switzerland with its beautiful snow covered Alps and lush valleys? How could anyone leave the neat row houses with flowers falling out of each window? This young man told me that Switzerland was like a state park. It was beautiful, but the rules and restrictions were so difficult you could not live. He said America was much like a wilderness, free and wide open. You can

Lisa Sturdivan
Dreamer - Habitat Owner

Mr. Hicks
Dreamer - Habitat Owner

Future Dreamers

One of my future dreams is to
help my nieces & nephew go to college.

Amber

Mariah

Lary

Amy

Lacy

do anything you wish here.

This same story was echoed by Etienne Gibbs, a friend of mine who left the Virgin Islands to live in the extremely small military town of Radcliff Kentucky. He told me you can only go so far in the islands, but here the possibilities are endless. Don't let the voices that tell you "things are bad" and "you can't make it" fill your mind. Listen to the voices that say, "This is a blessed time and a blessed place and you can achieve your dreams despite your problems."

One last story. Sue Thomas was born a normal child until she went deaf at age 18 months. She went through years of not being able to understand or speak. But Sue didn't listen to the negative voices. She listened to the voice of her teacher who said, "You can speak." Today, after years of work and struggle, Sue speaks. She speaks well enough that she gave a keynote address at the National Speakers Association recently. She has also learned to sing, and she closes her presentations with a rendition of "Silent Night." If this woman can overcome deafness to find a voice with which to speak and even sing, you and I can overcome our problems and find our voice with which to dream.

Success Breeds Success!

Find a small dream, something you know you can do and accomplish it. Then choose a little bigger dream, again something you know you can accomplish and complete this dream. This will build confidence in your ability to accomplish your dreams. Keep this practice up until you reach the big dream in your heart!

1. _____

2. _____

3. _____

4. _____

5. _____

6. _____

7. _____

8. _____

Mitsubishi 3000 GT

Tips for Entrepreneurs

1. If you can start your business in any of the many "Small Business Incubators" operated in every major city in America and run by the Chamber or city Economic Development Departments, you have a very good chance of succeeding. According to the United States Department of Commerce, 87% of all businesses started in these incubators between 1980 and 1991 are still in business today.

2. Start a business that will help people work at home. One in 10 employees telecommute at least 1 or 2 days a week. It is estimated that 48% of the labor force will be working at home by the year 2015. One major corporation claims it is saving $70,000,000 a year in real estate costs by having people work at home.

3. You are never too young! The National Federation of Independent Businesses found that people under age 35 started or purchased 1.9 million businesses in 1996. That was 43% of all new businesses started. Half of these people invested less than $4,000 and 3/4 started from scratch.

Section III

Making it work!

"Your words are the greatest power you have. They are the bricks and mortar of the dreams you want to realize. The words you choose are used to establish the life you live."
Croquette Sonia

Step 5
Harness the power of Words

So often I am asked 'so how do we get out of these prisons? How do I move from the circumstances I find myself in to the fulfillment of my dreams?' My answer is very simple, **"We speak our way out of our prisons and into the dreams we desire."** Let me explain.

Thomas Merton, a monk in Bardstown Kentucky, many years ago was translating an ancient Indian text and found a piece of prose that went like this...

If you sow a thought...you reap an attitude.
If you sow an attitude...you reap a belief.
If you sow a belief...you reap an action.
If you sow an action...you reap a habit.
If you sow a habit...you reap a lifestyle.
If you sow a lifestyle...you reap a character.
You can trace it all back to what you think about...
Choose your thoughts carefully.

Think about the last vacation you took. You and the love of your life were sitting on the couch one evening and the subject of vacation came up. "Where do you want to go on vacation this year?" was the simple question.

Then a thought hits one of you, "What about going to the beach?" If you like this thought you keep thinking about it. If you don't like the idea, you discard it and go on to something else. But letís say you like the idea, so you will mention it to your spouse. Your words to your spouse are simply a verbalization of your thought. So you had a thought and you sowed it in the form of a sentence to your spouse.

Then you began to form an attitude based on your thinking about the idea. You think about the price of going to the beach, whether or not you like the sun, and what you did on your last vacation, and your attitude is formed as to whether you want to go to the beach or not this year. If you or your spouse forms a negative attitude, you will stop this line of thought and begin to develop a new thought about where to head for your vacation.

If you have a good attitude about the beach, you then begin to form a belief about whether it is possible for you to go to the beach or not. This might seem like a subtle difference, but believe me there is a big difference between wanting to go to the beach and believing it is possible timewise and moneywise for you to go to the beach.

If you believe the beach would be fun and you believe you can afford it, then you begin to act on this belief. You pull down the map and select the beach. You make a couple of phone calls to check on airfare and you check with your boss to see what weeks you can get off work. The point here is that you begin to act on your belief.

If you have a good experience you may repeat this vacation. I know people who have gone to the same Florida beach every year for 30 years. They have created a habit and a lifestyle out of their actions.

The fascinating thing to me is -- you can trace the entire vacation back to the original thought you had sitting on the couch.

How many times a day do we go through this process? You have a thought....you either dismiss it or keep on thinking about it. If you dismiss it, nothing happens. You move on to your next meeting or idea. If you keep on thinking about your idea, you will quickly come to a decision saying, "I like this thought" or "I don't like it." This we call an attitude. If you like the idea, you will keep thinking about it and you will begin to form a belief saying, "Yes, this idea will work" or "No, this idea won't work." If you don't think the idea will work, you dismiss it and move on. If you believe the idea will work, you have to decide if the idea is valuable. A value is simply a belief you care about. If you value the idea, you very likely will act on the idea. If you have success with your action, then you will continue to act on that idea and you will form a habit. That habit over time will become a part of who you are.

Take a look at holding sales meetings at your office. Someone believed it was good idea. They thought about it and then suggested it to the big boss or the committee that works on it. After some more discussion, an attitude was formed saying, "Hey, this is a good idea." Then a belief was formed, "Yes, this will work." Then it became valuable enough for someone to put it on the calendar and set a time. If the sales meeting accomplishes what the originator thought it would, then s/he will plan another one. After a few meetings, it becomes a habit and a part of the culture of the organization.

The question comes, "How do we use this process for our good rather than by accident?" How do we use this process to get out of our self-imposed prisons? **We use words!**

What does a therapist or psychologist do when you go to them with a problem? They ask you questions to get you talking and they try to reframe the language you use to describe your problems. And by getting you to see the problem in a different light and by getting you to talk about it differently, s/he can help you grow.

Alcoholics Anonymous uses this method to help alcoholics. They get the person to admit they have a problem first. No progress can be made until the person first admits out loud with words they have a problem. Once this is done, then through education, prayer and companionship, they can help someone stay off the bottle.

Hitler used words to change the minds and hearts of the people around him and then his country. And he changed forever the face of the world with those same words. One of his famous sayings was, "If you tell a lie big enough and long enough, people will begin to believe it." If he did this in a negative way, can you and I do it in a positive way? Yes!

Years ago I read about a South American Indian tribe which had no known cases of stuttering. No one had ever stuttered in their history and no one stuttered in the then current population.

When the anthropologists finally translated the language of the people, they found no words in the language to describe stuttering. The experts concluded stuttering was a product of diagnosis. How many other diseases and habits do we possess because of the powerful suggestions of the words we use?

We can use words to direct the thoughts we have. These thoughts will then form our attitudes and beliefs, and we will then act on these beliefs.

When I realized my mother was wrong about my spelling, I began to say to myself, "I can spell." This statement was very laughable at the time, but I kept saying it, "I can spell, I can spell." Eventually I thought if I can spell, I had better improve my spelling. So I went to the book store and began to read books about spelling. And when I met with some success, this reinforced my belief even further. Today I can spell much better than I could a few years ago.

Our words can give direction to our thoughts and this begins the process that forms our attitudes, beliefs and ultimately our actions.

So how do we use our words to direct our thoughts and thus our actions? Well, there are seven ways...

1. Self-talk. Perhaps you have heard of this before, but each of us has an internal dialogue within our own heads. We need to get control of the words we use in our heads to speak to ourselves. The average person speaks at 200 words a minute. The average person thinks at 600 words a minute. It is therefore estimated we have 50,000 to 70,000 thoughts going through our heads each day. This cascade of thoughts, this internal dialogue is known as self-talk. Of what are those thoughts? Are your thoughts moving you forward or are they negative and moving you backward?

2. Psychological anchors. An anchor is a quote or picture that reminds you of your dream. You may have these in your office or on your desk, and when you read the quote, it reminds you of how much you want your dream. This is not magic or mysterious. It is simply a way to trigger the mind to think about your dreams. I love to tear out pictures of my dreams and place them in a dream book. When I review this book it reinforces my dreams in my mind.

Do the pictures on your walls remind you of your dreams or do they remind you of your past? Do the quotes you have on your desk make you laugh or do they inspire you to move forward?

3. Affirmations. Affirmations are one-sentence statements of what you want to be true. The problem is most of us affirm what we do not want to be true. We say things like "I can't lose weight on a diet" instead of saying "I weigh 113 lbs. in a firm healthy body." I suggest you write 3 affirmations for each of your dreams. Write an **"I am"** sentence, an **"I see"** sentence and an **"I feel"** sentence.

The **"I am"** statement states the idea in the first person. It helps this dream become yours instead of a dream you heard from someone else. It gets your heart, soul and mind into the action mode. *"I am a positive and exciting person."*

The **"I see"** statement helps you paint a picture in your mind of your dream. Psychologists tell us we move toward the picture we have in our heads. If you have a weak picture in your head of who you are, you will move toward that. The **"I see"** statement helps paint a strong positive picture of what you want in your mind. *"I see myself greeting people with excitement and enthusiasm."*

The **"I feel"** statement gets your heart and emotions involved in the process. As we will see later, nothing happens unless our feelings get connected to the words. *"I feel my best connecting with people."*

Scott Adams, the creator of the famous Dilbert cartoon, says, "To live big dreams you must first visualize them." Scott always wanted to be a cartoonist, but at age 30 he was no where close to his dream. So he started writing down his dream in a one-sentence affirmation. 15 times a day he would envision himself as a national cartoonist and he would envision a big -named cartoonist retiring. And it happened. "Don't ask me how, but affirmations do work." Today Scott uses the e-mails he gets from workers and the memory of his own postal worker father to get his Dilbert cartoon. Dilbert is syndicated in 1400 newspapers.

4. Mission Statement. The movie, "Dead Poets Society," has a poignant moment in it when the professor played by Robin Williams calls his young students around him and says, "Life is more than jobs and money. Sure we need doctors and lawyers and businessmen to keep society going, but what are we keeping it going for? Love, life, enjoyment are some of the reasons." And then he quotes Shakespeare, "The whole of life is a stage and the mighty play goes on so you can add a verse. What will your verse be?"

You are not here on this earth by accident, you are here by divine appointment. There is a reason God placed you here on this earth. To find this reason and to give your life to this end is one of the greatest joys in life. One way to find this meaning of life is to write a mission statement for your life.

A mission statement is a one-sentence statement of what you want to do with your life. When you answer the question "what would you do if you knew you could not fail," sometimes a theme emerges. Out of these dreams you can see some of what you like to do and the direction you want to set for you life. Can you now set that direction down in one sentence?

When I answered the question about what I would do if I knew I could not fail, I came up with the ideas of owning 100 acres of land, of starting a non-profit organization and I wanted to become a philanthropist. (A philanthropist is someone who gives money away for a foundation.) When it came time for me to write a mission statement I looked carefully at my dreams of starting a non-profit organization and of being a philanthropist. I thought, "I want to help people, but I don't want to do it like everyone else does. I want to be creative and I want to make a real meaningful difference." So my mission statement came out like this. "To create a positive difference in the world in which I live." This is a one-sentence statement that states my desire to help the environment and people and do God's work. It is broad enough to allow me to be creative and to change and grow as I go.

A speaker friend of mine, Rich Wilkins, has a statement: "To effect the attitudes of people worldwide."

One of the best mission statements for a business I have ever seen is by BellSouth, "Bring people together through communication..." Each department has a mission statement that begins with those words and then is specified for that department. For example the marketing department says, "We bring people together through communication by having and implementing an effective marketing plan."

A mission statement sometimes comes quickly, sometimes it takes months or years to perfect. Take a few minutes and try to write a statement for your life.

_____

_____

_____

_____

_____

Don't be afraid if this comes slow. It does for many people. Think about it, work with it, discuss it with your spouse, and reflect back on your dreams. Come back to this question often to try to get your mission down to one sentence. This is a very powerful way to get your words to begin to shape the direction of your life.

5. Vision Mission statements can be cold and vague. Sometimes it is helpful to draw a picture of your mission statement. This picture of the fulfillment of your mission statement can provide color, emotion and excitement to your overall mission. It can provide a fleshing out of your intentions. I call this picture a vision.

If you were to draw a picture of the perfect life, the perfect home, the perfect job, the perfect day, the perfect financial picture, what would it look like? What would your life look like if you could live out the mission statement you have for your life?

The vision for my own life is not a hard picture to paint. One morning in the not too distant future, I awake without an alarm, read for an hour and write for 2 hours. I head to my office where I make my phone calls and attend to the paper work. During this time I sell 10,000 books and schedule two speaking engagements. It is then time to head off for a speaking engagement before a large group of adoring fans. That night I spend time with my family and work on a dream project to help other people. As I reflect on my day, I realize I'm on pace to earn $250,000 a year, I am helping 50,000 people a year follow their dreams, my house is paid for and I am able to sleep soundly only to arise the next morning and create a positive difference in the world in which I live. This is simply a picture of what my mission statement might look like when completed.

Some people say this picture is too dreamy, too perfect and unrealistic. I will admit that compromises are made in life. But too many of us lower our dreams and compromise from a compromise. I'd rather compromise from perfection than from a compromised position.

I only use my vision as an example. What is truly important is what your life would look like if you knew you could not fail. Take a moment and draw that picture.

6. Dreams Oh, here is the fun part! Now it is time to spell out the things you will have to do to make that mission statement and vision come true. You can call these projects or goals. I call them dreams. You may have thousands of dreams you would like to accomplish, but for now write down the 4 or 5 major dreams you need to accomplish to make your vision and mission statement come true.

What are the dreams you need to do to fulfill the mission of your life?

1. _____
2. _____
3. _____
4. _____
5. _____

7. Goals, Actions, Objectives

Have you ever known someone who had all types of lofty dreams, but they never seemed to do anything? They never moved beyond what they are currently doing to put feet to their dreams. This will never do for me. I want to be known as someone who has accomplished dreams not just talked about them. That is what this chapter is about. Breaking down those lofty dreams to a point where they can be accomplished easily.

For each dream you have, list the 4 or 5 goals you will need to accomplish to fulfill that dream. Then for each goal list the 4 or 5 activities you will need to do to accomplish that goal. If necessary break down that activity to the 4 or 5 tasks you need to do to accomplish that activity.

These steps are here to help you. Only use the ones you need, but breakdown that lofty dream into small enough steps that you can start today with step one and reach that dream step by step.

Let me provide a quick example. My mission statement is to create a positive difference in the world in which I live. In my vision of how this plays out in my life, I picture myself working on dream projects that actually help people, thus creating a positive

Mission Statement

A one sentence statement of your vision.

Vision

A picture of what you want your life to be.

Dreams   Dreams   Dreams

1. *Goal*
     -Objective
       --Task

2. *Goal*
     -Objectives
       --Task

1. *Goal*
     -Objectives
       --Task

2. *Goal*
     -Objectives
       --Task

1. *Goal*
     -Objectives
       --Task

2. *Goal*
     -Objectives
       --Task

difference in my world. Well, one of the dream projects I have worked on for several years is to own 100 acres of land. This dream project would be a great investment for my retirement, it would be a great place of recreation for my family and it would help preserve some wilderness which in turn can help the environment and the next generation. It worked well into my mission statement by helping my family and the next generation. So how do we go about buying 100 acres of woodland? Well first, we set a dream of owning 100 acres of land. Then we break this dream down into manageable goals.

Goal 1:   **Find 100 acres of land for sale.**
    Activity 1:   Phone local real estate agents.
    Activity 2:   Read the local papers looking for possible sites.

Result: <u>SUCCESS: Found 110 acres of land with a 50-acre lake for sale at $299 an acre.</u>

Goal 2:   **Raise $33,000 to buy the land.**
    Activity 1:   Develop a plan that would convince bankers, family members and myself this is a good idea, we can afford it and we can use the land for good purposes.
    Activity 2:   Show the plan to family members.
    Objective 1: Write a speech that is persuasive enough that the members of my family would want to be a part of this project.
    Task One: Set up a personal meeting with key players in my family.
Result: <u>SUCCESS: Two members of my familyagreed to fund the entire project.</u>

I could carry this on for pages, but you get the point. The dream is broken down into very very small steps so I can follow through on each of them. This type of plan helps you break a lofty dream down into manageable parts. And it worked. It took several years to complete, but my wife and I bought 110 acres of land for $299 an acre. I personally did not put a penny into the deal. (At the time I had no money.) The land sits on a 50-acre lake and is a beautiful retreat. We have since added an additional 100 acres to this farm and recently another 90 acres have come up for sale.

And it can work for you. Take any lofty dream you have and break it down into very small parts. This will be a great exercise to see if you are serious about your dreams. Most people are not that serious. They want to talk about dreams, they want to aspire to dreams, they want to go to seminars, etc., but they are not serious enough to write down their dreams, break them down into manageable parts and begin to work on them.

The reason is simple. As long as their dreams are vague and out there, they don't have to be responsible for achieving them. They don't have to be accountable for making them happen. Don't let this happen to you. Follow your dreams to their fulfillment.

This process will take the words you speak and place them into a system that will organize your thinking and your actions. And you can literally speak your dreams into reality. I know this works because I have used it to accomplish my own dreams. In December of 1998, we dedicated the brand new Habitat for Humanity house. The young family moved into the house on December 14th. My Christmas was made complete when I got a card from that young family thanking me for my work. The card said, "There is no place like home for the holidays."

Tips for Entrepreneurs

1. Don't watch TV! Harvard Economist Juliet Schor found the more TV you watch the less money you save. Each hour of TV reduces your annual savings by $208. Her theory is many popular TV shows promote an upscale lifestyle that few people can afford to live. Plus every advertisement you watch encourages you to spend money.

2. Help people downshift. According to the program "Downshift your Lifestyle" by WHAS TV (2/21/97), 64% of people surveyed said they would accept less pay if they could do what they really want to do.

3. Discipline is the key. Psychologist David Moore, PHD says, "Lack of discipline is the great enemy of the dreamer. People set out great plans, but then they get bored after the first two or three steps and give up on their dreams."

*"The great end of life is not
knowledge but action."*
Thomas H. Huxley

Step 6
Dream Book

What would happen if you went to the grocery store without a shopping list? You would forget half of what you needed and you would end up with stuff you don't need. The same is true if you go through life without a dream list. You forget to do half of the stuff you wanted to do and you will end up doing things with your life you never intended.

My best friend in high school fell into this trap. He was an extremely smart and talented young man, but he ended up going to college with no particular plan. And just like picking up stuff in a store you don't want, he got into things he never intended to do with his life. While at college he started smoking dope, exploring a strange eastern religion and playing jazz music all night and thus he flunked out of college his first semester. After college he fell into different odd jobs and eventually he picked up a wife and two kids he really didn't want. He told me one day he had really wanted to study philosophy and teach, but his life had turned out very different than he intended. He started out without a plan and he ended up not doing the things he wanted to do and doing a lot of things he didn't want to do.

The same can happen to you if you don't write down your dreams. So let's develop a Dream Book that will detail all your dreams. A book that outlines your mission statement, that paints the vision of this mission statement, that enumerates the dreams you have for your life, that lays out the plans you have for fulfilling those dreams and the affirmations that will help you accomplish those dreams.

At your local office supply store, purchase a show file. This is a portfolio with plastic pages inside into which you can insert 8.5x11 pieces of paper. On the first page, print out your mission statement. You may want to be creative in how you express this mission statement, but do it now!

On the second page draw your vision of you life. Do this with words first and then if you can, do it with a drawing or a picture of some kind.

On the third page list out the dreams you will need to do to accomplish your mission and vision statements. There will usually be 4 to 8 dreams. The number is not important. What is important is to list out all the things you will need to do in order to fully accomplish the reason you were placed on earth.

On pages 4-8, break down each of those dreams into small manageable steps. Write out the goals, actions and objectives you need to achieve to make each dream come true.

On each of those pages 4-8, write the 3 affirmation statements for each of the dreams. Read these every morning and every evening as they will help you program your mind.

This book will become a source of strength for you. When you are hurting and lost wondering what to do next, you can find answers in your Dream Book. As you accomplish the dreams you set down, you will find a great deal of inspiration knowing you are a dream maker.

Dream Ideas!

I have dream ideas that pop in my head all the time. I have listed a couple of these ideas here. Use them if you can. What are more valuable are the ideas that pop into your head as you read these ideas.

1. The Japanese have developed fiber optics to the point they can pipe sunlight underground and use sunlight to grow vegetables. Why hasn't someone attached a lamp to the end of that fiber optic tube and given us natural sunlight in our homes? It would even be a better trick if you could attach the original end of the fiber optic cable to a solar panel and give us a sunlight lamp for free. There are parts of the world with no electric plants that would love to have solar powered lamps.

2. Why hasn't someone done for jobs what Habitat for Humanity has done for housing? Take an individual off the welfare roles, provide them a mentor, a low-wage job sweeping floors or something and then provide a systematic job ladder that will eventually take them to a $30,000-a-year job. This would be a project big enough to attract money, people, corporations and non-profit help. In the end, everyone wins.

3. Build 50 Habitat for Humanity houses in your city. It costs $40,000 to build one Habitat house. If you could get 50 churches to agree to raise $5,000 a year for 4 years, this would pay for half of the houses. Then get 10 corporations to donate $25,000 a year for 4 years. This project is a project big enough to get people excited and it would help your entire community.

4. While appliances are not in use, keep electricity in the wall sockets. I saw a news report recently that said if you unplugged an appliance after using it, it would cut down on your electric bill. Well, invent a plug end that would replace the plug at the end of my TV cord that would guarantee me energy savings each year by blocking this electricity escape. On a recent trip to Europe, I found on and off switches on each electrical outlet. So, I know items have already been invented, but I have never seen anything like them in America.

*"The emotions may be endless.
The more we express them, the more
we may have to express."*
G.K. Chesterton

Step 7
Emotions

I have emphasized the power of words to shape our attitudes, then our beliefs and then our actions, but words cannot do this work alone. The words we speak through our affirmations and mission statements must be backed by powerful emotions. Words in fact mean nothing unless we give meaning to them. We give them meaning with our emotions.

For example, I could say "Your are worthless" and this statement may not upset you at all. It may mean nothing to you. But if your mother or father or boss said this to you right after you had messed something up, you may indeed feel they were right. You may give a great deal of meaning to their words. But the words themselves, whether written or spoken, have no value. They only have value when we give value to them.

This is also true of our dreams. We can write mission statements and speak affirmations about our dreams for the next 100 years, but if we do not place emotions behind the words we speak, they will do no good.

Good examples of this, are people who claim they want to be rich, and tell me their dream is to be a millionaire. In my opinion the word millionaire has taken on a mythical or romantic notion in this country. People think, "If I were a millionaire, I would be rich, I would never have to work again and I would have enough money to take care of my family and health and travel all I wished."

Can you see how this type of thinking is romantic? People claim a dream of being a millionaire, but in reality they want all their problems to be taken away. This dream of being a millionaire is a simple figure of speech for a vast undefined dream of having all my problems taken away. It's very easy for the words behind this type of dream to have little meaning in your own mind. Deep down you know all your problems cannot be taken away, therefore, you know you can't achieve this dream and you have little incentive to work toward that dream.

When I run into someone like this, I always ask them to tell me a specific number it would take for them to be rich. They usually say "one million dollars" to which I retort, "If you put that in the bank and earned 8%, you would make $80,000 a year and the government would take 50% which would leave you $40,000 a year. Is that what you want?" They usually respond, "Well, that's a good start, but I am making more than that now. Being a millionaire would mean a step down for me." This simple conversation proves they have not thought about how much money they need in order to be rich which was part of their original dream.

The dream of being rich must be defined far more clearly than just throwing around a figure of speech. It must be defined in such a way you believe it is possible to achieve it and your emotions can be connected with the dream. For me, being rich does not mean not working. It means having the cash flow to do what I want to do. I dream of earning $250,000 a year, while working 30 hours a week. Eventually this will lead me to a $2,000,000 net worth. Can you see how specific this dream is? Believe me I am now at a position to believe this dream is possible and this gets me emotionally excited about following this dream.

Psychologists tell us there are four basic emotions: sad, mad, glad and fear. There are maybe thousands of variations of these emotions but these are the basics. What words can you use to bring emotion, feeling, value or meaning to your dreams?

Here is a list of emotional words you can use to get started:

excited	suspicious	envious
confident	stubborn	ecstatic
aggressive	regretful	curious
determined	relieved	confused
discouraged	sad	bored
enthusiastic	sorry	cautious
happy	puzzled	anxious
hopeful	paranoid	sure
innocent	pained	bashful
interested	negative	apathetic
loved	jealous	annoyed
love-struck	lonely	angry
peaceful	mischievous	shy
optimistic	miserable	hurt
proud	humiliated	hostile
satisfied	hysterical	helpless
shocked	guilty	frightened
surprised	frustrated	embarrassed
thoughtful	fearful	alienated
undecided	disgusted	
withdrawn	disappointed	

*"I dare to take responsibility,
for my sake not yours."*
From the ancient text

Step 8
"I'm in charge.
I don't care what you say!"

You have heard the old saying, "If at first you don't succeed, try try again." Well, our society has changed that saying to, "If at first you don't succeed, fix the blame fast." We want to put the blame for our mistakes on everything under the sun except ourselves. If we don't make enough money, it's the boss' fault. If we don't have good enough health, it's our parent's fault. If we spill our coffee, it's the restaurant's fault. One essential step for making dreams come true is to take 100% responsibility for everything that happens in your life. If you are having money problems, instead of blaming the boss, blame yourself. If you were more valuable to the company, then they could pay you more. If you have a difficult marriage, ask yourself, "Who said 'I do'?" Yes, situations and people change, but we have to begin to accept our role in creating the circumstances in which we live.

For several years I taught a Bible study class for single people. When someone decided to stay home or go to Shoney's for breakfast instead of coming to my class, I considered it my fault they didn't come to my class. Some might say this is a very harsh way to look at life, but I knew that taking personal responsibility for people being in my class was the only way I could have control over the situation. If I simply threw my hands up and said, "Oh well, that's just the way things are," then I would have given up control for the attendance at the bible class to circumstances. If I took personal responsibility for someone being in the class, then I would have some control and could work on a solution. What I did was try to make my class so good that people would rather be at that class than be at home in bed. I wanted to make a personal relationship with everyone in the class so they could feel personally connected to me and to the class. This type of personal responsibility turned my class into a very very strong class that did a lot of good for a lot of people.

This is the type of personal responsibility I want you to take over every aspect of your life including your dreams. Say it with me....

If you're overweight, whose fault is it?.... Mine!
If you're struggling with debt, whose fault is it?.... Mine!
If your'e struggling in a bad marriage, whose fault is it?... Mine!

The only way you can take control over the outcome of your situation is by taking personal responsibility for your circum-stances. Now that you're taking responsibility for the circum-stances you're in, you can begin to change them. It may require very very small steps at the beginning, but that's OK. You're on your way.

"I know your car was totaled, but we can't sue the manufacturer of a tree."

"*I always wondered why somebody doesn't do something about that. Then I realized I was that somebody.*"
Lily Tomlin

Step 9
Motivation

Motivating yourself and the people who work with you is another important component of making dreams come true. There are two basic motivating instincts found in people, "the hope of gain" and "the fear of loss." People can be enticed to move by the hope of gaining money or prestige or you can move someone because they fear they will lose something. There is a big debate as to which of these motivators is more powerful, but most psychologists, as much as we hate to admit it, seem to come down on the side that the fear of loss is more motivating. How much more feverishly and focused do you work if you seriously think you are going to lose your job or your house? This same intensity will come if you are being confronted by a mugger and actually fear for your life. Because of the fear of loss, adrenaline rushes into your blood and causes your mind to focus intently on the problem. This same adrenaline gives you enormous power and energy to do things. This is why you hear the stories of elderly ladies picking up cars to save a young child. This fear of loss is especially good during times of war or the threat of violence.

The problem is the fear of loss is so limiting. As soon as you get out of danger your body stops secreting adrenaline. It has a drive to rest from all the physical exertion you have expended. This motivation will only take you out of danger. It is the more powerful motivation, but it is very limiting.

Many sales people and professional people find themselves living a middle class lifestyle, because fear motivation is the only motivation they understand. Once they reach the salary where they can make their mortgage payment, drive a decent car, take a two week vacation, go out to eat once a week and send their kids to college, they seem to stop moving up. You see their basic needs are covered and they run out of motivation to move up. So they stop in their career or their sales activity around $35,000. (This may sound extremely low to some of you who live in large cities, but it is the average income in America.) In the personal coaching I do, I can help a client move from $18,000 to $30,000 or from $50,000 to $100,000 a lot easier than I can help someone go from $30,000 to $50,000. The motivation for gain is still valuable, we simply need to learn to get the same intensity for our dreams as we do for our fears.

Have you heard the old adage, "You can lead a horse to water but you can't make him drink."? Well that is true, but you can take a horse, run him around in circles for 3 hours and when you lead him to the water he will drink all the water you have. The same is true with our dreams and the people we manage in our family, projects and businesses. We can build the desire inside so that people will want to accomplish. This is done in 3 ways.

1. **Vision.** Yes, we are back to this vision thing. People think in pictures and they must have a picture of what the dream or project will look like when it is finished.

2. **Believe it is possible.** This is where most sales organizations fail. They give people the rah rah routine, but if the person fails the first few times they try to sell something and if they meet with mediocrity the next 6 months of their career, they soon stop believing this dream is possible. There is nothing more fatal than believing something is not possible. So not only must you and your people see a vision of the dream completed, you must also believe you can get there.

3. **Desire to accomplish that dream.** This is the 3rd piece of the puzzle. If you have a picture and you know you can get there, you must want to go there for your reasons. People will not do things for your reasons, they do them solely for their reasons. You can't motivate people for the good of the company. You will build desire because it is good for them. The people must emotionally want to accomplish a certain dream or they will not do it even if they have a good picture and know they can achieve it.

Here are 9 emotions and motivators as identified by Napoleon

Hill in his work, "Think and Grow Rich." Can you match each of these motivations to your dream?

1. Love
2. Sex
3. Desire for material gain
4. Desire for self preservation
5. Desire for freedom of body and mind
6. Desire for self expression and recognition
7. Desire for Life after death
8. Desire for Revenge
9. Fear

"Don't let opinions of the average man sway you. Dream and he thinks you are crazy. Succeed and he thinks you are greedy. Pay no attention. He simply doesn't understand."
Robert G. Allen

I Built a House for $200

When I finished a speech recently, an old geezer came up to me and asked, "You're real good son, but does this stuff really work?" All I could do was tell him my story.

In 1984, I found myself in what I call the flood. I was down on my luck, broke, unemployed and living on borrowed money. While trying to put myself back together, I picked up a tape by Dr. Robert Schuller which asked the question, "If the world were perfect, if you knew you could not fail, what would you do?" With this question I began to dream. I dreamed of owning 100 acres of land, of getting married, of owning a nice home, of owning a sports car and starting my own business and a non-profit organization. I wrote all of these dreams down in a book.

Within six years all of these dreams came true. Not every detail came true, but the essence of the dreams came true. I had married a beautiful young lady, had formed my own speaking business, had bought 100 acres of land, had lived one year in Tokyo Japan and had even incorporated a non-profit organization. The accomplishment of these dreams made me a believer in the power of a Dream Book.

As I continued my research into how our bodies, minds and spirits work, I began to learn the power of words to express our ideas, shape our attitudes, beliefs, and actions and therefore our futures. Once I discovered this, I tested the idea on a couple of very small dreams, like learning how to play a game and taking a trip to go hang gliding. With the confidence of these two successes I began to form the system of mission statement, vision, dreams and goals.

When I combined the Dream Book, responsibility and emotion to this process, dreams just really started to pop for me. I used this process to spend two weeks in St. Petersburg Russia, to buy a $46,000 car for $14,900 and to spend 3 weeks in Wales, Germany and France this past fall.

All I did was ask the question, "What would I do if I knew I could not fail?" Then I wrote down those dreams and worked toward their completion. I don't know about you, but I have always had this romantic notion of riding a motorcycle across the United States. This is probably some romantic notion inspired by the Easy Rider movie and the songs of Woody Guthrie, but in my mind it was the ultimate symbol of freedom. But there was a problem as there is with all dreams. To take a slow and easy ride across America would take 2 or 3 months and several thousand dollars. At this stage in my life, I can't afford to do this, so what is a dreamer supposed to do? Then one night it hit me, "Maybe I can't ride the entire United States, but I bet I can ride the entire state of Kentucky." So I devised a plan. Since Louisville is somewhat in the center of the state, I could ride to the western border and back in one weekend and then turn around and do the eastern side the next weekend. In 1998 I rode my motorcycle across the state of Kentucky twice. Just a dream. Just a dream that came true.

This year I plan to ride the states of Indiana and Tennessee. I may not be able to ride the entire country at once, but I can ride most of it one state at a time.

I have a dream, like many people of being rich. But as I examined my heart, I realized I didn't need to be rich today. What I really wanted was to be rich when I retired. So I devised a plan to acquire $1,000,000 worth of real estate, let the renters pay off the real estate and own it free and clear when I'm 65. This dream is still in process. We have just reached the $800,000 mark. It is, however, coming true.

But these are just material dreams; they do not help me become a philanthropist, which is my life-long dream. The non-profit organization I had set up to help people was just sitting there. I had put some money into it, but it really wasn't doing anything. Then Edgardo Mansilla asked me if I could raise some money to buy cars so his people could get back and forth to work. Well this request to a dreamer was like a bone to a dog. I jumped all over it. I made 5 phone calls, raised $1,000 and bought two cars. I fixed them up and gave them to people who had jobs but needed transportation to and from work.

Then I got to thinking, could I do this on a regular basis? Could I get 10 people to each put up $200 twice a year and use the money to really make a difference with people in need? My $200 may not do much, but multiply it times ten and $2,000 is enough to do something. I spoke to 15 people and ten of them said, "Yes." This group became known as the Heroes Club. We have provided the cars I spoke of, we have provided 10 new computers for a computer lab that is teaching job skills in 4 languages and we have started endowments for the Kentucky Brain Injury Association and for an inner city organization that is sending kids to college. I have become a philanthropist for $200.00!!!

About 2 years ago, the heroes club decided to give $2,000 to Habitat for Humanity. While sitting at my desk, I got to thinking, "I need to dream higher." So I called Habitat and discovered that if I raised $17,500, they would match it with $17,500 and we could build an entire house. Again, this idea to this dreamer was like a bone to a dog. I jumped all over it. I found out that the Baptist churches in my city had never been the official sponsors of a Habitat House. So I called 10 of them, told them I had already raised $2,000 from the Heroes club and asked each of them to give $2,000. Nine of them did. In 1998 we provided labor and money and built a Habitat for Humanity House. The house was completed in December and dedicated on my birthday December 14th. A young lady, who had been at the same job for 9 years, and her two young children moved in just before Christmas. They sent me a card that said, "There is no place like home for the holidays." My contribution to this project was $200 and leadership. I have become a philanthropist for $200.00!!!

This process has also been able to help other people. Darryl Rowe, a computer specialist and a friend of mine, took this material, hit the books hard, worked through a couple of jobs and ended up doubling his salary over a 3 year period. You can read about Darryl's dreams at his website www.iglou.com/homepages/darrylr.

Dean Nicklas is a good friend and a great graphic artist. Dean created the cover and cartoons for this book. A few years ago when Dean and I started working on some projects together, I kept telling him how talented he was and how he was vastly underpaid for the talent he possessed. Dean worked through a couple of jobs and has increased his salary by 50% in just a few months.

Jack Small is a sales manager for a large network marketing company, who has always wanted to sing. Last year Jack's income was 3 times the average American's income, but that's not good enough for this dreamer. By dreaming high Jack has been able to develop his singing and speaking skills and this year he will double his income over last year. Jack says it so well, "I know a blind sales manager. I know a sales manager who has no hands. I myself am tone deaf, but still I sing! Your dreams can come true, the only question is how bad do you want them."

Kay Seiskar is a friend of mine from the National Speakers Association. In 1989 she and her husband had a goal of being debt free, children free, and living free. They turned that dream into a goal by putting a 10-year time frame on the dream. In 1998 with their kids out of the house and their debts paid off, they sold their house and set out on the open road in a RV one year ahead of schedule. They speak in various areas of the country, do ministry with various church groups and share their story of how you too can be free.

All of these dreams did not happen overnight, but all of this did happen to me in the 15 years since my flood.

"15 years!" the old geezer interrupted me. "Well, I thought you were going to tell me it only took you 2 or 3 years. I was going to call you lucky or a fluke if you did it in only 3 years. But 15 years, heck anyone could become a millionaire and done all that stuff in 15 years."

"Yes, that's exactly right!" I replied. "That's my message! Anyone can achieve the life they wish if they simply dream."

I'm not stopping

My dreams are not stopping here. I want to build a killer web site, www.dreamhigh.com. I want to increase my income to $250,000 a year while working 30 hours a week. I dream of living to 125 years of age and still be teaching, speaking and writing. I want to have a net worth of $1,000,000 by the time I'm 43 years of age. I want to increase my land holdings to 1,000 acres. I have at least 4 more books to write.

I want to leave 3 one-million-dollar endowments to help people before I die. I have 4 nieces and one nephew I want to help go to college. Can all this come true? You bet. Will it come true exactly as I have planned? Well, we'll see. I am certainly looking forward to the ride.

The dreams I have set for myself you may consider low or you may consider them too high or very idealistic, but the dreams I have set are what I want to do with my life. Now it is time for you to dream. Just remember you are more than you know and you can achieve more than you currently believe. Dream high and then work to make those dreams come true.

A word of wisdom...

One day I was facing some real difficulties with my dreams and was wondering if I could ever accomplish the things I had set out to do. I sauntered down to a bench overlooking a lake surrounded by beautiful pine trees. An old man in plain clothes and a long beard came walking up and asked if he could sit down. "Sure," I responded and we chatted for a while. Feeling I could trust this man and sensing he was perhaps wise, I asked, "Can I accomplish the dreams I desire..."

"YES!" he loudly interrupted me in mid-sentence. **"Now, tell me your dreams!"**

Here's to your dreams,

Conway

Conway

Section IV

Motivational Quotes

The following quotes are for you to use in your speeches and meetings. Read one each day and try to apply its truth.

A dream is just a dream, if it's only in your head.
If no one gets to see it, it's just as good as dead.
Stephen Sondheim

Many receive advice, only the wise profit by it.
Syrus Latinmimi writer

Most people have the will to win,
few have the will to prepare to win.
Bobby Knight

Don't lose your head, it's the best part of your body.
Jimmy "The Greek"

Action may not always bring happiness;
but there is no happiness without action.
Benjamin Disraeli

By your own soul learn to live.
If men thwart you, take no heed,
if men hate you, have not a care.
Sing your song, dream your dream,
and pray your prayer.
Unknown

First we make our habits, then our habits make us.
Charles Noble

Demanding that greatness be turned loose within us eventually
releases something greater than we are.
H.L. Menckn

Most men die from the neck up at the age of 25,
because they stop dreaming.
Ben Franklin

Dreams are a reflection of what you value and believe.
Rich Wilkins

Dream in a pragmatic way.
Aldous Huxley

Men are not prisoners of fate, but only prisoners of their own minds. Franklin D. Roosevelt

Most dreams of glory are safe because we never venture
to put hem into practice.
Charles Curothe

Men of reason have endured; men of passion have lived.
French Philosophy

Only the passion for great dreams can elevate
the mind to great things.
French Philosophy

Every thinker put some portion of the stable world in peril.
John Dwey

Man is only great when he acts from passion.
Benjamin Disraeli

Of the billionaires I have known, money just brings out the basic
traits in them. If they were jerks before they had money, they are
simply jerks with a billion dollars.
Warren Buffet

One secret of success in life is for a man to be ready for his opportunity when it comes.
Benjamin Disraeli

Money doesn't bring happiness, though it has been known to
cause an occasional smile.
Herb True

Opportunities are often disguised as hard work,
so most people don't recognize them.
Ann Landers

The quality of a person's life is in direct proportion to
their commitment to excellence, regardless of
their chosen field of endeavor.
Vincent T. Lombardi

Small opportunities are often the beginning of great enterprises.
Demosthenes

It is a funny thing about life: if you refuse to accept anything but
the best, you very often get it.
Somerset Maugham

All things are difficult before they are easy.
John Norley

**The price of greatness
is responsibility.**
Winston Churchill

Man's mind once stretched by a new idea, never
regains its original dimensions.
Oliver Wendell Holmes

Society needs its dreamers. Those willing to follow visions, work
for new things and accomplish.
Anonymous

There is great meaning in life for those who are willing to journey.
Jim England

Passions are the gates to the soul
Author unknown

By annihilating the desires, you annihilate the mind.
Everyone without passion has within him no
principle to action no motive to act.
Author Unknown

We are told never to cross a bridge till we come to it, but this
world is owned by men who have "crossed bridges" in
their imagination far ahead of the crowd.
The Speakers Library

Use the talents you possess. The woods would be
very silent if no birds sang except the best.
The Speakers Library

If you have a new car, would it matter if you did not put the key in
and turn and push on the peddle. The same is true with your
dreams, they have no value by themselves.
Author Unknown

If you get close to people, you will catch their dreams.
Anonymous

Following his childhood dream of drawing comic strips, a young
man was advised by an editor in Kansas City to give up drawing.
He kept knocking on doors, only to be rejected. Finally, a church
hired him to draw publicity material. Working out of an old
garage, he befriended a mouse who ultimately became famous. The
man was Walt Disney, his dream was DisneyWorld,
and his friend was Mickey Mouse.
Walt Disney

There is nothing like a dream to create the future.
Victor Hugo

When you have a dream, you've got to grab it and never let go.
Carol Burnett

Dreams have only one owner at a time.
That's why dreamers are lonely.
Erma Bombeck

It takes a lot of courage to show
your dreams to someone else.
Erma Bombeck

A dream only reflects the dreamer's thoughts.
Jonathan Eleazar

What marks a dreamer is dedication to an ideal, a dedication so strong that it rejects outright the complacency of those who prefer the status quo and insists there has to be another way.
Author Unknown

Every battle is won or lost before it is fought.
The Art of War

Ships are safe in harbor, but that is not what ships are for.
Country Song

The best way to predict the future is to invent it.
Author Unknown

Those who want to reap the benefits of this great nation must bear the fatigue of supporting it.
Thomas Payne

A coach is someone who can give correction without causing resentment.
John Wooden

Everything great that has ever happened to humanity since the beginning has begun as a single thought in someone's mind. And if anyone of us is capable of such a great thought, then all of us are capable of that thought.
Yanni

The highest reward for a person's toil is not what they get for it,
but what they become by it.
John Ruskin

The worst bankruptcy in the world is the person who
has lost his enthusiasm.
H.W. Arnold

If a man is called to be a streetsweeper, he should sweep streets even as Michelangelo painted or Beethoven composed music or Shakespeare wrote poetry. He should sweep streets so well that all the hosts of heaven and earth will pause to say, here lived a great streetsweeper who did his job well.
Martin Luther King Jr.

You will become as small as your controlling desire;
as great as your dominant aspiration.
James Allen

Be careful what you set your heart on, for it will surely be yours.
Ralph Waldo Emerson

Seeds of great discoveries are constantly floating around us, but
they only take root in minds well prepared to receive them.
Joseph Henry

Pythagoras was misunderstood. So was Socrates, Jesus, Luther,
Galileo, Newton and every pure and wise spirit that ever took
flesh. To be great is to be misunderstood.
Emerson

Don't let the opinions of the average man sway you.
Dream and he thinks you are crazy.
Succeed and he thinks you are greedy.
Pay no attention, he simply doesn't understand.
Robert G. Allen

To know and not to do is not yet to know.
Zen Saying

Knowing is not enough, we must apply.
Willing is not enough, we must do.
Goethe

Ultimately we know deeply that the
other side of every fear is freedom.
Marilyn Ferguson

If one advances confidently in the direction of his own dreams, and endeavors to live the life which he has imagined, he will meet with a success unexpected in common hours.
Henry David Thoreau

The best way to become an old dog is to stop learning new tricks.
Anonymous

A generous man will prosper
Proverbs 11:25

Genius is one percent inspiration and ninety-nine percent perspiration.
Thomas Alva Edison

Don't confuse wishes with wants.
When you want a thing, you go out and get it.
When you merely wish for something,
you just wait for it to come to you.
Jack Klein

In all things, it is better to hope than to despair.
The ancient text

Anyone who keeps learning remains young, regardless of their age.
Unknown

You might not always get what you want, but you
always get what you expect.
Charles H. Spurgeon

When it's all said and done there is usually more said than done.
Unknown

I have known a great many troubles - most of
which never happened.
Mark Twain

It is the set of the sails, not the direction of the wind
that determines which way we will go.
Jim Rohn

Reading is to the mind what exercising is to the body.
Sir Richard Steele

Associate yourself with people of good quality, for it is
better to be alone than in bad company.
Booker T. Washington

We are what we repeatedly do. Excellence, then,
is not an act, it is a habit.
W.B. Prescott

It is a funny thing about life: if you refuse to accept anything but
the best, you very often get it.
Somerset Maugham

All things are difficult before they are easy.
John Norley

Destiny is not a matter of chance, it is a matter of choice.
Unknown

The highest reward for a person's toil is not what they get
for it. Even if you're on the right track, you'll
get run over if you just sit there.
Will Rogers

**He who has a why
to live can bear
almost any how.**
Nietzsche

Hold a picture of yourself long and steadily enough
in your mind's eye, and you will be drawn toward it.
Napoleon Hill

The end of wisdom is to dream high enough
to lose the dream in the seeking of it.
William Faulkner

Just don't give up trying to do what you really want to do.
Where there are dreams, love and inspiration,
you can't go wrong.
Ella Fitzgerald

To accomplish great things, we must not only act
but also dream; not only dream, but also believe.
Anatole France

It is difficult to say what is impossible, for the dream of yesterday
is the hope of today and the reality of tomorrow.
Bob Goddard

When we can't dream any longer we die.
Emma Goldman

Dreaming is an act of pure imagination, attesting in all men a creative power, which if it were available in waking would make
every man a Dante or a Shakespeare.
H. F. Hedge

No one should negotiate their dreams. Dreams must be free to fly
high. No government, no legislature, has a right to limit your
dreams. You should never agree to surrender your dreams.
Jesse Jackson

"Mrs. Keller, is there anything worse than being blind?"
She replied, "Yes, to be able to see and not have a vision."
Tony Robbins

Whatever you can do
or dream, you can
begin it. Boldness has
genius, power and magic
in it. Begin now!
Goethe

Dreams are the touchstones of Character.
Henry David Thoreau

No man becomes suddenly different from
his habit and cherished thought.
Commander Joshua L. Chamberlain

The greatest piece of real estate you
own is the 6" between your ears.
Unknown

I don't design clothes, I design dreams.
Ralph Lauren

All men dream, but not equally. Those who dream by night in the
dusty recesses of their minds, wake in the day to find it was vanity:
but the dreamers of the day are dangerous men, for they may act
on their dreams with open eyes, to make them possible.
T.E. Lawrence

My dream is of a place and a time where America will once again
be seen as the last best hope of earth.
Abraham Linclon

I thank God I live in a country where dreams can come true,
where failure is sometimes the first step to success, and
where success is only another form of failure if
we forget where our priorities should be.
Harry Lloyd

There are those who will say that the liberation of humanity, the
freedom of man and mind is nothing but a dream. They are right.
It is the American Dream.
Archibald MacLeish

The key to success is simple. Make people dream.
Gerald deNerval

If you want your dreams to come true, don't sleep.
Yiddish Proverb

Nothing happens unless first we dream.
Carl Sandburg

Commit yourself to a dream. Nobody who tries to do something great but fails is a total failure. Why? Because he can always rest assured that he succeeded in life's most important battle; he defeated his fear of trying.
Dr. Robert Schuller

Don't part with your dreams. When they are gone you may still exist, but you will have ceased to live.
Mark Twain

Some people look at the world as it is and ask why. I dream of worlds that never were and ask why not.
George Bernard Shaw

Goals are dreams with deadlines.
Diana S. Hunt

Most dreams of glory are safe because we never venture to put them into practice.
Charles Curothe

Small opportunities are often the beginning of great enterprises.
Demosthenes

If you do not ask, the answer is always "no."
Owen Laughlin

All men of action are dreamers.
James G. Huneker

I am only one, But still I am one.
And because I cannot do everything that I can do.
Edward Everett Hale

We know what we are, but know not what we may be.
Shakespeare

Compared to the cost of ignorance the
price of education is cheap.
The ancient text

To share often and much,
...To leave the world a little better,
...To know even one life has breathed easier
...because you have lived,
...That is to have succeeded.
Ralph Waldo Emerson

Shoot for the moon. Even if you miss it you
will land among the stars.
Les Brown

Mind is the master; power that molds and makes. Man is mind and evermore he takes, the tool of thought and shaping what he wills, brings forth a thousand joys, a thousand ills. He thinks in secret and it comes to pass. Environment is but his looking glass.
James Allen

Many people talk like philosophers and live like fools.
H.G. Bohn

Every great achievement was once considered impossible.
Author unknown

The voice of the intellect is a soft one, but it does not rest until it has gained a hearing. Ultimately, after endless rebuffs, it succeeds. This is one of the few points at which one may be optimistic about the future of mankind.
Sigmund Freud

Nature of men is always the same. It is their habits that separate them.
Confucius

I would rather see a crooked furrow than an unplowed field. I would rather attempt something great and fail than to attempt nothing and succeed.
Dr. Robert Schuller

A little philosophy inclineth a man to atheism. A depth of philosophy bringeth a man's mind about to religion.
Bacon

Asking is the beginning of receiving. Don't go to the ocean with a teaspoon-at least take a bucket so the kids won't laugh at you.
Jim Rohn

Don't set your goals too low. If you donít need much, you won't become much.
Jim Rohn

It's better to have common sense without education than to have education without common sense, though it's best to have both.
Anonymous

If thou art a man, admire those who attempt great things, even though they fail.
Seneca

Dreams are made up mainly of matters that have been in the dreamer's thoughts during the day.
Herodotus

When one teaches, two learn.
Robert Half

A Dreamers prayer
Lord, maker of desires and dreams, hold me close to the heart of
thy spirit so that by the grace of thy almighty hand I will be able
to fulfill the reason you placed me here on this earth by following
and accomplishing my dreams.
Conway Stone

If you don't risk anything, you risk even more.
Erica Jong

There is no sin except stupidity.
Oscar Wilde

**The unexamined
life is
not worth living.**
Socrates

I never worry about action, but only about inaction.
Winston Churchill

When you come to a fork in the road - take it.
Yogi Berra

The brilliant moves we occasionally
make would not have been possible
without the prior dumb ones.
Stanley Goldstein

What you do speaks so loudly that I cannot
hear what you say.
Ralph Waldo Emerson

I find it useful to remember, everyone lives by selling something.
Robert Louis Stevenson

When work is a pleasure, life is a joy.
When work is duty, life is slavery.
Maxim Gorky

There is nothing either good or bad
but thinking makes it so.
Shakespeare

What really matters is what you do with what you have.
Shirley Lord

They call you stubborn when you fail,
but persistent when you succeed.
Anonymous

One ought to hold onto one's heart; for if one
lets go, one soon loses control of the head too.
Nietzsche

The easiest kind of relationship for me is with ten
thousand people. The hardest is with one.
Joan Baez

Life is something that happens to you
while you're making other plans.
Margaret Millar

Our duty is to be useful, not according to our
desires but according to our powers.
Henri F. Amiel

The main dangers in this life are the people
who want to change nothing.
Lady Nancy Astor

Only a fool tests the depth of the water with both feet.
African proverb

The pessimist may be right in the long run, but the optimist has a
better time during the trip.
Anonymous

If we desire one thing and expect another, we become like a country at civil war - two sides warring with no one winning.
Conway Stone

A mistake at least proves someone stopped talking
long enough to do something.
Conway Stone

Every dreamer works in violate disagreement with their times.
Conway Stone

We must nurture our dreams like we would a child. They are God given and just as precious. Without ambition how would a child learn to ride a bicycle, play an instrument or whistle? We deny the spirit of God when we as adults settle for less than our dreams!
Conway Stone

He who expects much receives much.
He who expects little receives little.
He who expects nothing is seldom disappointed.
Conway Stone

Dreaming is not an accident.
It is not a wistful idea you hope will come true.
Dreaming is not the stuff of long-haired hippies
wistfulling running along a beach. No,
dreaming is a sophisticated tool used by the elite of our
society to make themselves and this world a better place.
People like Millard Fuller, founder of Habitat for Humanity,
Warren Buffet, Col. Sanders and Walt Disney all started with a
dream. The dreams started small but like the water that formed
the great Grand Canyon, dreams are POWERFUL!
Conway Stone

Our greatest foes' are within.
Cervantes

To accomplish great things, we must not only act, but also dream;
not only plan, but also believe.
Anatole France

The first idea the child must acquire is that of the difference
between good and evil.
Maria Montessori

I always wanted to be somebody, but I should have been more specific.
Lily Tomlin

Not admiring a mistake is a bigger mistake.
Robert Half

Money never starts an idea. It is always the idea
that starts the money.
Owen Laughlin

They may kill the dreamers, like they did Kennedy,
King, Ghandi and Lincoln. But I am convinced that
as long as you and I follow our God given dreams,
they will never kill the dream.
Conway Stone

There is nothing either good or bad
but thinking makes it so.
Shakespeare

The opposite of love is not hate, it's indifference.
The opposite of art is not ugliness, it's indifference.
The opposite of faith is not heresy, it's indifference.
And the opposite of life is not death, it's indifference.
Elie Wiesel (Oct. 1986)

One doesn,t discover new lands without consenting to
lose sight of the shore for a very long time.
Andre Gide

A life spent making mistakes is not only more honorable
but more useful than a life spent in doing nothing.
George Benard Shaw

Restlessness and discontent are the first necessities of progress.
Thomas A. Edison

We choose our joys and sorrows long
before we experience them.
Kahlil Gibran

Thought is the blossom; language the bud;
action the fruit behind it.
Ralph Waldo Emerson

What we need are more people who can
specialize in the impossible.
Theodre Roethke

What you want to do, and what you can do,
is limited only by what you can dream.
Mike Melville

**The future belongs to
those who believe in the
beauty of their dreams!**
Eleanor Roosevelt

If you can dream it, you can do it. Always remember that this
whole thing was started with a dream and a mouse.
Walt Disney

"The shell must break before the bird can fly."
--Tennyson

What really matters is what you do with what you have.
Shirley Lord

They call you stubborn when you fail,
but persistent when you succeed.
Anonymous

A ruler isn't always straight.
Robert Half

Dreams are made up mainly of matters that have been in the
dreamer's thoughts during the day.
Herodotus

Dost thou love life? Then do not squander time,
for that is the stuff life is made of.
Benjamin Franklin

Love doesn't make the world go 'round; love is
what makes the ride worthwhile.
Franklin P. Jones

The great end of life is not knowledge but action.
Thomas H. Huxley